Contemporary violence

MANCHESTER
1824

Manchester University Press

This book is dedicated to my parents, Howard Clemison Moore and Hilary Moore

Contemporary violence
Postmodern war in Kosovo and Chechnya

Cerwyn Moore

Manchester University Press

Manchester and New York

distributed in the United States exclusively
by Palgrave Macmillan

Published by Manchester University Press
Oxford Road, Manchester M13 9NR, UK
and Room 400, 175 Fifth Avenue, New York, NY 10010, USA
www.manchesteruniversitypress.co.uk

Distributed in the United States exclusively by
Palgrave Macmillan, 175 Fifth Avenue,
New York, NY 10010, USA

Distributed in Canada exclusively by
UBC Press, University of British Columbia, 2029 West Mall,
Vancouver, BC, Canada V6T 1Z2

British Library Cataloguing-in-Publication Data is available

Library of Congress Cataloging-in-Publication Data is available

ISBN 978 0 7190 9566 5 paperback

First published by Manchester University Press in hardback 2010

This paperback edition first published 2014

Printed by Lightning Source

Contents

Preface

Books are in many senses like journeys; they never represent the efforts of a single person, but are rather a product of, and are greatly enriched by, many conversations and encounters. These conversations and encounters, and for that matter the conversations still to come about Kosovo and Chechnya, the Balkans and the North Caucasus, war, social networks and interpretive IR, will, I hope, be enhanced in some small way by this book.

So to trace the journey of this book: the writing of my Ph.D. at Nottingham Trent University between 1999 and 2004 laid the foundations for this analysis. It was the culmination of a long process of learning, stretching back through many years studying in the libraries and wandering the corridors of Staffordshire and Nottingham universities in the 1990s.

Further sections of the book were written across a number of extraordinarily eventful years for me, from 2004. The work on Kosovo and indeed interpretive and qualitative approaches to International Relations grew out of reflections on my doctoral research, aided greatly by the support, encouragement and generosity of my supervisors Dr Chris Farrands, and latterly Professor Heikki Patomaki. Both were always ready to offer helpful advice and encouragement, and have since become good friends.

I was pleased I could connect my interest in studies of war, post-Soviet security and IR at Nottingham Trent University, and this was helped enormously by professional comments and thoughtful words of advice from Professor Lloyd Pettiford, Dr Roy Smith, Dr Ruth Griffin, Olwyn Ince and Chris White. More recently, thanks are due to Alan for helping me format the book. Thanks also to my external examiner Professor Martin Shaw who aided my understanding of particular conflicts and the social forces which impact on war. Thanks to both Iver Neumann and Roland Bleiker who, in more recent years, have both encouraged me to pursue my research. There of course many others, too numerous to mention here, who helped through-out my years of study. My doctoral studies could not have been completed without research in the Balkans, in Kosovo and Macedonia in 2001. Thanks to the former KLA fighters, members of the Serbian and Albanian Diaspora population, local politicians, NGO officials, scholars and journalists who I either interviewed, or who offered guidance and thoughts on my work. Finally here a note of special thanks must go to the team who helped me travel from Macedonia back to Pristina on 18 May.

I am thankful to the British Academy for the financial support I secured in 2003, and also in 2005; both enabled vital fieldwork in Russia and the Caucasus. This book is a product of that financial support. My experiences in the South Caucasus up on the Chechen border were helped enormously by my fixer, interpreter and friend, Koba. A quick coffee with Koba in a cafe in Tbilisi led to a chance meeting and a new set of travelling companions, colleagues and friends.

Many thanks to the photographers Mark Johnson and Glenn Dearing: looking forward to more adventures in the near future; keep those shutters rattling, keep taking those prize-winning photographs and hope you enjoy the read!

So many people showed me kindness and friendship, when planning and during my research visits to Russia and the Caucasus throughout 2004 (April, May–September) and in September 2005. Amongst others, a personal thanks to Natalya, Anna P., Volodya, Malcolm, Valeri, Natasha, Tom, Zarina, numerous peoples from the UN, Andy V. and the OSCE. But I must add a special thank you to Madina and family; looking forward to more coffee and working with you in the future.

Similarly Sweats and family; on many occasions I shared those dark days with you throughout Basayev's terror campaign in 2004, so many thanks for putting up with a somewhat jittery academic, particularly after Beslan, and keeping me up-to-date with all the transfer news about Liverpool FC. Lastly here, the broader body of work simply could not have been completed without the guidance, and more importantly the friendship of two people, Professor Stephen Chan and Paul Tumelty. Their generosity – munificence even – greatly enriched my understanding of IR and political violence. My heartfelt thanks to both: this book could not have been written without your help.

There are two or three other groups of people who I need to thank, par-ticularly because encounters and conversations with all have enhanced the analysis in this book. First and foremost, thanks to the journalists, aid-work-ers, writers and news editors who I have spoken to, or travelled with over the years. Thanks to one and all at the Frontline Club, where, over many years, I have either met and/or interviewed people, or stayed before embarking or returning from trips to Russia and the Caucasus. At the BBC thanks to Mark, Steve, Damian, David and Murad who generously gave up their time to speak with me about Kosovo and Chechnya. Particular thanks also to another group of writers and journalists, the roll-call of which includes James, Sophie, Janine, Natasha, Tony, Sanobar, Sebastain, Anna, Maria, Tom and Anne N. Thanks to Sonia at Noor Photo Agency and, of course, to Stanley Greene; your award-winning and arresting images of different parts of the world continue to amaze me, and continue to drive me to write about the North Caucasus. Colleagues at the University of Birmingham including Laura Shepherd, Christopher Finlay and Edward Newman kindly offered comments and thoughts on an earlier version of the manuscript, which enabled me to significantly revise the arguments and analysis in the book. In addition, thanks to a host of other academics who have offered thoughts about the two regions and encouraged me to pursue my work on Kosovo and Chechnya; the list is, as ever, incomplete, but it includes Galina, Moshe, Brian G.W., Marie Bennigsen-Broxup, Svante, Anna Zelkina, Charles Blandy, Jon Coaffee, Emil Souleimanov, Lee Bosher, David Fletcher, and lastly, and most importantly, Dr David Barnard-Wills – your invaluable comments, criticisms and advice meant 'the book' could finally be completed. Officials including David Owen have been very helpful, as have others including Lord Judd. I am grateful to those working for charities and aid organisations, including Satanay and John, and Tomas at PW. I also owe a debt of gratitude to the Chechens and Russians who I have spoken to, interviewed and become friends with over the time spent researching this book. The book and the research was compounded, even dislocated somewhat, by an injury to my leg, ankle and heel in 2007. Manchester University Press was more than understanding, graciously allowing me more than the three months I needed to stand on two feet again. The book is a product of their encouragement, and patience. Thanks also to the two anonymous reviewers who offered thoughtful comments on the original proposal, while I owe a debt of gratitude to Professor Karin Fierke, who kindly reviewed a draft of the manuscript offering generous, supportive and extremely helpful comments at very short notice.

Acknowledgements abound in any preface designed to foreground analysis of this sort, particularly when drawing on a broad body of previously published research. The work on Chechnya, the 'picture economy', narrative and literary global politics was originally presented at BISA in December 2004, and was since published in *Global Society*, Vol. 20, No. 2 in 2006, in an article 'Reading the Hermeneutics of Violence: The Literary Turn and Chechnya'. Parts of this article provide the basis for Chapters 1 and 5, while other bits of the article have been worked into the book as a whole. More general theoretical work in the Introduction and Chapter 1, exploring interpretive IR – and aspects of the aesthetic turn and poststructuralism – formed the basis for parts of my doctoral thesis. Other aspects of this work – particularly its theoretical tenor – resulted from extended conversations with both Chris Farrands and Stephen Chan. Some of these conversation have since been picked up and transformed into an edited collection entitled *International Relations and Philosophy: Interpretive Dialogues* (London: Routledge, 2010).

My work on the transformation of Chechen resistance, internal radicalisation and the broader historical and cultural dynamics which shaped the insurgency in the North Caucasus continues, although parts of this analysis did appear in an article, 'Combating Terrorism in Russia and Uzbekistan', in the *Cambridge Review of International Affairs*, Vol. 20, No. 2. Some aspects of this article appear in rewritten form in Chapter 6. Moreover, my work on the shifting nature of the Chechen resistance, as it formed, evolved and changed, particularly in its use of radical tactics including suicide attacks and in the role of social networks and foreign fighters, formed the basis of two articles, co-authored with Paul Tumelty.

Both provide the backbone of my ongoing research, which may one day form a manuscript focusing specifically on the insurgency in the North Caucasus. The first article entitled 'Foreign Fighters and the Case of Chechnya: A Critical Assessment', was published in *Studies in Conflict and Terrorism*, Vol. 31, No. 5 in 2008. Even though I have only used small portions of this article in Chapter 3, the thoughts contained in it, which were originally drafted in 2004, provide the basis for some of the broader ideas in the book. The second article, 'Assessing Unholy Alliances in Chechnya: From Communism and Nationalism to Islamism and Salafism', was published in *The Journal of Communist Studies and Transition Politics*, Vol. 25, No. 1 in 2009. I have used portions of this piece which focuses on the development of the insurgency in the North Caucasus, the role of military jamaats and internal radicalisation, throughout the book. In addition, I draw on a series of other shorter articles, commentaries and discussion pieces throughout the book published in *International Criminal Law Review*, *Prague Watchdog*, *Central Asia and Caucasus Analyst* and through the *Jamestown Foundation* terrorism monitor.

I continued to read and draft my findings on Chechen suicide attacks throughout 2003, and having undertaken the fieldwork in 2004, I drew these ideas together in a series of presentations at, amongst other places, BISA in December 2004, at the ERSC workshop on suicide terrorism in January 2005 and at ISA in Chicago in 2006. This batch of early work provides the basis for parts of Chapter 8. This work has since been substantially reworked, indeed radically altered, forming the basis of a forthcoming paper on Chechen suicide attacks and strategy which will be published through *Europe-Asia Studies*. Indeed I grateful acknowledge the assistance of *Europe-Asia Studies*, which also allowed me to use aspects of a 2008 review article, subtitled 'Putin's Post-Colonial War(s)' here.

Above all though, my gratitude goes to the members of my family. Mum, Dad and Del, apologies for getting caught up in the events in 2004 and 2005, thanks for all the moral, financial and emotional support, and indeed your patience in dealing with me. It is to you that I dedicate this book.

Introduction: alternative approaches to violence in International Relations

This introductory chapter seeks to identify the key theoretical literature in International Relations (IR) which can be used to explore contemporary violence. Albeit in an exploratory fashion, this chapter will touch upon the work of scholars concerned with meaning in IR. Equally, the chapter recognises the broad body of work on conflict and new wars.[1] This work illustrates how paramilitaries, international aid groups, human rights organisations, transnational media-corporations, militias and inter-governmental organisations are all involved in contemporary war. Drawing on this premise, this book argues that conventional theoretical accounts of war in IR are no longer adequate – if indeed they ever were. On the one hand then, accounts of war in Kosovo (1998–1999) and Chechnya (1999–2002) are interesting because both were, somewhat obviously, constituted by post-Cold War readings of global politics. On the other hand, both examples also provide an empirically rich source of information, shaped by a broader post-Communist narrative, and influenced, historically at least, by the collapse of the Ottoman Empire and era of Great Power politics. And of course, both conflicts were shaped by their locations on the borderline between different geopolitical regions.

I will of course return to these two themes in the next two chapters, but at this point it is necessary to note another general body of work which influences this book, and indeed studies of conflict; narrative accounts of global politics.[2] In fact, I would argue that the work of war reporters, human rights activists and former combatants interact with the processes of globalisation, mixing the field of study, to generate alternative stories of war. The way that conflicts are captured and inscribed – as well as the way they are iterated, performed and portrayed – mean that war occurs in a variety of public and political spaces. That is to say, ideas about the development of alternative modes of apprehending IR are important where they touch upon and locate

1

theory as a sense-making activity. A concern with narrative is useful then, precisely because it serves to highlight the possibility that there might indeed be different stories to tell. And these stories shed light on the local milieu, the social relations and cultural forces which shape accounts of war. Combined with this, partaking in war became part of a narrative of belonging and connectedness, with iterations of heroic behaviour in battle inscribing communal and kin groups linking this with a social account of identity in ritual, ceremony and myth. These rituals and ceremonies form part of a chain of events which allows people to locate the self historically.

In the introductory remarks to his Wiles lectures, published under the title *Philosophers of War and Peace*, the historian W.B. Gallie argues that:

> We can perhaps best come to appreciate the distinctive structure of the international problems, centred on the nature and causes of war and possibilities of peace, by studying the reaction to it of a cluster of thinkers who were forced to face it at a time when it seemed very much simpler than we now know it to be. Kant, Clausewitz, Tolstoy and founding fathers of Marxism all saw the international problem in what we today might well consider to be simplistic terms. But this does not mean that they showed themselves simpletons in their handing of it.[3]

Of course Gallie demonstrates the importance of these writers, who, far from being simpletons, help us to understand war. In doing so, Gallie demonstrates the importance of what we today would call inter-textual studies. He also draws attention to the role of imaginative, political, fictional and philosophical studies of war through narrative. In very different ways writers such as Clausewitz,[4] or in the context of this book, Ivo Andrić[5] and Leo Tolstoy,[6] provide interesting markers which help us read, understand and interpret different approaches to war. Even though his work was presented to a different audience, the same sort of judgement and the same process of filtering underpins the arguments herein. Historical knowledge, analytical rigour and an awareness of literary sources help to situate war, to overcome existing silences which, I would argue, are echoed in IR theory. That is to say that IR theory, partly due to the process of abstraction, often denudes war from the very narratives and stories, myths and legends, as well as the local or regional dynamics which produce it. It may be said then, that accounts of war resonate today, not least because Chris Hedges points towards fragmented political contexts, recognising that war occurs in different locations and in different forms.

While it is often linked to somewhat mundane everyday practices, routines and performances which produce a stable expectation of identity, groupness and otherness, be it through the life of the family or one's work-life, these reference points are constitutive of narrative identity. The repetition and recognition of these characteristics of narrative identity are not only constitutive and productive, they not only enable a sense of identity to form, but these characteristics are also amendable to interpretive and hermeneutic approaches to global politics.

Stories of war and peace: locating Hermeneutic Studies

In order to explore the different approaches to the study of war I turn here to a body of interpretive work which, I will argue, helps to link area studies and social networks with studies of narrative identity. When taken together, these three overlapping themes underpin the insight in the book. In trying to reconcile these areas of interest, detailed political and strategic themes are placed aside so as to enrich concerns and ask new questions about the hermeneutics of contemporary violence.

The adoption of an interpretive stance issues in an awareness of the rich field of hermeneutic enquiry, 'the continual process of mediation by which that which is societally transmitted (the tradition) lives on'.[7] Of course hermeneutics has many forms.[8] In IR this approach has some overlaps with interdisciplinary approaches in, for instance, anthropological, linguistic, filmic, or literary representations of life.[9] Within many of these studies it is obvious that war is a radically diverse phenomenon. A commitment to hermeneutics as a method does not commit one to deny any reality as much as it commits one to treat claims to reality with great caution.[10] Hence, this book is not 'hermeneutic' in a thoroughgoing sense, but in a distinctive, cautious and yet interpretive sense. It does not take a 'radical' or 'strong' poststructural stance nor critique this standpoint which disrupts meaning, and which would more appropriately reflect the work of, for instance, Baudrillard.[11] Instead, by acknowledging the need to explore war through cultural and social theory, the analysis offers a way to overcome the plethora of problems associated with undertaking a purely abstract or anthropomorphic view of IR; it is to see war as a hermeneutical problem.

In explaining the constructions and representations of (and in) war, the analysis recognises that there are always ambiguities and contradictions in interpretation, and that interpretation is itself a construction of meaning.[12] Thus the analyst, who is also a narrator of a kind, has no objective position, no 'Archimedean point' or overview, from which to view the subject of study. This might lead to a radical relativism in which it is possible to say nothing with any certainty. But as Ricoeur, amongst others, suggests, the dialogue through which we struggle to make sense of a conflict of interpretations is itself a way of narrowing down what might be sensible or appropriate ways of 'reading' the text.[13] Indeed, much of Ricoeur's work is designed to counter the apparent conclusion that phenomenology does not allow us to engage with 'real' experiences such as suffering, and on this, from the 'other side' of the argument, there is some convergence of sorts with more recent writing by some writers in the Anglo-Saxon tradition[14] who have criticised empiricism without abandoning some kind of engagement with practical experienced realities (what Husserl calls, the 'life-world').

Some recent theoretical contributions have engaged with hermeneutics in a rewarding manner.[15] This work has provided a useful array of theoretical interventions based upon questions of meaning, and an application of hermeneutic inquiry linked to the empirical 'life-world'. Nonetheless it is the work of Paul Ricoeur which I draw on when turning to founding events, so as to enrich narrative and literary accounts of IR. Furthermore, his ideas on inscription and an archival trace provide a useful way to reconcile reading and writing, history and memory, seeing, as he does, the interpretation of literatures as a problem for hermeneutics. In this way Ricoeur offers an applied hermeneutics coupled with research committed to the real world.

Another feature of the analysis that follows is the recognition of the plasticity of violence, shaped predominantly by the analysis of war in the postmodern age. This is significant because war is being increasingly characterised by a circumscribed artificiality: a virtualisation and effects-based character. But does this mean that war itself is changing, or is it the context or lens through which we read and write about certain wars that is changing? Does the virtualisation of violence, and the concomitant functions of mimesis mean that the distance between the reading and writing of war has changed? Does the idea of a virtualisation of war, embodied and articulated in, for example, some of the work of Baudrillard and Virilio, focus on theoretical questions of authentication and not the realities of conflict?

The argument then is to recognise that a central feature of the Kosovan War for NATO at least, was that it was fought in electronic and informational spaces using an air-campaign framed by list-based targeting, changing the very experience of violence for some of the participants in the conflict. However, this is only one reading of the Kosovan war. Until now the two main conditioning axes of war, state and non-state violence, have continued to provide the lens through which conflict is theoretically conceptualised in IR. While this theoretical focus helps to offer insight into security, securitisation and strategy, my aim here is slightly different, seeking to explain what is going on, and why. But this does lead me to make a theoretical claim about 'postmodern' war, echoing the first usage of this label by Fredric Jameson in 1984.[16] War as a distinct phenomenon, eschewing defined characteristics, is more accessible, but more difficult to explain as a multi-dimensional phenomenon; hence the adoption of postmodern as a prefix.

It should be added that postmodernism, while providing a basis for research in important and adequate ways, does not provide the kind of methodology that an empirical or positivist approach would; and, for reasons of consistency, it should not be expected to do so. It is possible to articulate reasons and arguments for following a line of enquiry without having a single linear form of argument based on a single set of foundational epistemological and ontological assumptions. Indeed, if the most important single element in a postmodern approach is the rejection of foundational claims to know, then knowledge claims have to be made in a more self-critical, more elliptical and more cautious manner.

Postmodernism (at least of the kind which informs this study of war) is above all a form of scepticism about the claims of foundational thinking rather than a particular programme of knowledge or set of methodological claims. In so far as the structure of the book represents a series of forays into the material (each chapter being a separate expedition) rather than a one-way linear narrative, even the structure of the analysis reflects this concern. Thus the book should be read as a series of explorations of the main themes, albeit a series which is organised in a logical way rather than a story with a straightforward 'beginning–middle–end' format. Although this is no longer a particularly distinctive approach in itself, having existed in IR literature since the early 1990s, it remains unorthodox and challenging. The first chapter of the book offers a preliminary discussion of different narrative approaches to war, before introducing the two cases Kosovo and Chechnya in Chapter 2. Chapter 3 builds on the preliminary historical themes identified in Chapter 2, so as to examine regional dynamics and trans-local accounts of identity. Chapter 4 illustrates how the forces of globalisation and late modernity have facilitated a change in some aspects of contemporary war. Then, in Chapter 5 the analysis returns to stories of war in the Balkans and Caucasus, before moving on in Chapter 6 to look at criminalisation. The goal of Chapter 7 is to link stories with some aspects of the recent turn to emotionality, before addressing narratives and social networks in Chapter 8. The final chapter and the Conclusion draw the analysis together, reflecting on Kosovo and Chechnya and postmodern war.

Meaning and International Relations

With regard to the form of poststructuralism and the approach to issues concerning knowledge/discourse used in this book, it must be recognised that the understanding of language and knowledge is not just about the epistemological dimensions (the nature of truth claims) but is also about the ontological status of knowledge/language. In this way, language can be seen as a means of (pre-) structuring meaningful social practice rather than a transparent instrument mirroring objective reality. This position differs from the mainstream approaches which highlight empiricism, positivism and formal modes of inquiry as foundational and essentialist. In addition, this highlights a weakness in mainstream theories that seek to posit hypotheses and theories based on the premises of positivism and empiricism alone. The form of poststructuralism used here does not cross the Rubicon, so to speak, and engage directly with quantitative studies, but it does retain an awareness of the significance of detailed empirical and historical work.

It is also significant to recognise the role of communication in the construction of meaning, when turning to poststructuralism. Classical philosophers have tended to consider speech to have priority over writing, but, as this book suggests, labelling and meaning can arise as a result of the confluence of alternative representational processes. Seeking to reconceptualise meaning in IR, the poststructural project challenged both the modernist project and the end-sum epistemological notion of reason. Indeed, both Derrida and Foucault addressed questions of giving speech and writing meaning in complementary, yet slightly different ways. When assimilated, these forms of communication help construct meaning and it is this point, that meaning can be constituted through the process of communication that the book takes from their work on language. I hope that this echoes, in some way, the application of poststructuralism (deconstruction) and hermeneutics (interpretation) outlined in other recent work on IR theory.[17] Nevertheless, this raises further questions about meaning and the study of war.

This appropriation of hermeneutics and a reading of narrative help to question the research techniques, concepts, historical provenance, political referents (states) and theories adopted by conventional approaches in IR. In one sense therefore, it could be said that a limited conceptualisation of modern Western war has emerged in IR theory, which incorporates a variety of professional, organised and inter-state themes. Alternatively, it could be suggested that wars are not primarily inter-state and are also very rarely fought by similar forces using similar tactics; rather they are more commonly fought by asymmetrical forces, often explored in accounts of ethnic and civil war[18] which are not organised hierarchically. However, this form of war implies a changing location of political violence in relation to the state. Of course it is true that sub-state violence is not new – for example the Vietnam War was fought amongst the civilian population. Nonetheless a re-evaluation of this form of conflict could be seen as one way to move analysis forward, even if it requires a more refined historical and contextual approach to bolster interventions associated with, for instance, Mary Kaldor's account of new wars.

The relative informality of sub-state violence suggests that the organisational forms and borders of conflict are also shifting. As a result, what, where, how and by whom wars are fought become more engaging questions, drawing attention to, amongst other things, a strategic reading of the spectrum of contemporary violence from war to terrorism.[19] The attempt to form a legal definition needs to clearly represent the personalised, psychological and generative nature of conflict. Accordingly, a simple spatio-temporal, pseudo-legal explanatory definition of war, or the description of a value-laden representation not only acts as a misleading precedent for future conflict, but is also constitutive of our interpretation of war as a concept in IR. This process is inherently preconditioned and politicised by the practice of power. Conversely however, the argument here engages with the plurality of representations, locations and differing experiences of violence, so as to analyse the slippage between modem, late modern and postmodern war, by drawing on a poststructural ontology and its phenomenological roots. Phenomenology is the investigation of the way that representations, emotions, objects, images, experiences and ideas appear or are present in our consciousness.

Husserl states that 'In straightforward world experience we find human intentionally related to certain things, animals, houses, fields etc, that is, as consciously affected by these things, actively attending to them or in general perceiving them, thinking about them, planning and acting in respect to them.'[20] Therefore, a phenomenological approach looks at the object in 'itself' and examines the experiencing of events. Husserl's earlier work, especially *Logical Investigations*,[21] forms the basis of a series of debates about how we can understand social action. His earlier, more optimistic work, suggests that we can understand how people's intentions shape their actions, and how their perceptions and understanding of the world provide a logic of social action, which works in contradistinction to both the Kantian idealist tradition and the utilitarian positivism of British empirical social science, exemplified by writers such as Bentham and Mill.

Husserl's work does not provide a very satisfactory basis for social research for reasons which were analysed in a series of subsequent debates initiated by his successors. His work appeared to ground a method of argument, which was of great importance, but which put too much emphasis on two elements his critics found difficult to accept. Firstly, although he appeared to shift away from a rationalist account of human behaviour, for many of his critics he did not move far enough; secondly, his account of intentionality was seen to be flawed. His most profound philosophical critic, Heidegger, shaped the emergence of continental philosophy in developing these points at great length. More succinctly, and perhaps more clearly, Schutz developed an account of Husserl's work, which sought to deal with these criticisms and to integrate Husserl's writing with the understanding-based approach to knowledge in Weber's sociological writing.[22] Schutz's *The Phenomenology of the Social World*, first published in 1932, had a great impact both on more recent writers on phenomenology in particular,[23] and in sociological theory. More specifically, there is a direct influence from Schutz's work to critical theory and interactionist or constructivist social theory (including forms of constructivism in IR), whether or not it is acknowledged there.[24] Other writers whose work is shaped by phenomenology, and who contribute to the debate include Jean Paul Sartre[25] and Levinas,[26] who reacts fiercely against Heidegger's influence while remaining within the phenomenological 'family'.

It is not the purpose of this book to do more than briefly introduce these debates, since phenomenology is itself a very broad set of arguments. What is more important is to establish where I stand in relation to particular arguments within these debates, since they provide a source of the methods as well as the intellectual orientation of the analysis which follows. This will be done in subsequent discussion, partly in Chapter 1 and partly, where more appropriate, threaded into the book as a whole. Even so, the influence of phenomenology is particularly important, since it influences directly the analysis here, and the writers in IR who have brought their work into global politics through hermeneutics.

Finally, a further strand of IR, which draws attention to aesthetic, literary and artistic sources, is employed here, so as to draw on a form of interpretivism which may enrich our analyses of war, in both its abstract and empirical form. There are a number of reasons for this; first, to offer a stretching of the methodological turn, located in the cultural and social, but informed and transformed, through a reading of hermeneutic phenomenology concerned with language(s), symbol(s), inter-subjectivities and expressions; second, it is to draw on the grafting of hermeneutics onto phenomenology, particularly in the work of Ricoeur, precisely because hermeneutic phenomenology seeks to explore symbolic expressions, the unlayering of the 'experiential significations of these expressions',[27] and thirdly to re-engage with a movement beyond disciplinary boundaries and across differing levels of analysis. The reason for this is because Kosovo and Chechnya are marked by a need to explore 'interpretation'. As Don Idhe notes in his introduction to Paul Ricoeur's *Conflict of Interpretations*, the task, then, is to examine beyond the surface of meaning, because it 'may "hide" or "conceal" or at least "contain" a less obvious depth'.[28] As such hermeneutics is concerned with deciphering the plurality of meanings, and does not rest on studies of power relations or deconstruction alone. In this sense, war in both the Balkans and Caucasus has a deep-rooted meaning, shaped by waves of history, linked in part to materialism but also formed by the interaction of stories of war with late modernity and globalisation.

While I fully accept that each of the traditions – hermeneutics, phenomenology, postmodernism and poststructuralism – have been refined and developed in very different ways, it seems to me that they each provide a set of theoretical approaches which can be used to interpret and analyse contemporary violence. Hermeneutics (which is concerned with meaning and the interpretation of texts); phenomenology (which focuses on questions about how things are represented); postmodernism (which is read here as a form of scepticism that questions foundational meaning); and its close cousin poststructuralism (which embraces deconstruction), are all broadly read as useful traditions which may be used to approach how meaning is apprehended, inscribed, storied and interpreted. These four traditions help to guide the reader through several different layers of meaning, connecting the analysis that follows to – amongst other things – questions about story-telling and social networks, emotions and history.

Evidently though, there are tensions between these four strands of thought and it would be remiss not to recognise these here. Hermeneutics – particularly in its Gadamerian form – focuses on the interplay between the fusion of horizons, which leads to a conversation or dialogue between a whole and elements of a text, action or object. The observer is part of this process, but for critics this leads to an argument, associated with the hermeneutic circle, which is considered logically self-enclosed. In contrast here, the process of questioning, the dialogue, play and exchange of ideas is viewed as an iterative process, which leads to a set of interpretations which make texts more intelligible. That is to say that war has a mysteriousness, and yet has discernible features. War can be patterned and plotted – and it is sometimes framed by linear accounts of history and stories which simply unfold. And these narratives of war are amenable to hermeneutics which explores the 'continual process of mediation by which that which is societally transmitted (the tradition) lives on'.[29]

In contrast the offshoot of poststructuralism known as deconstruction is often presented as a challenge to, or rebellion against interpretive theories, and hermeneutics more generally. Deconstruction attempts to break free from questions of meaning, so as to establish a radical uncertainty of meaning in language. It does so by reading the text against itself, thereby exposing and questioning the root meaning of words. After identifying and exposing the fundamental conceptual oppositions which words rest upon – speech–

writing, natural–cultural, masculine–feminine – deconstruction then turns to destabilise these meanings, and highlight their inherent limitations and inadequacies. It seems to me, however, that the rigorous focus on deconstruction alone, particularly in some branches of poststructural IR, has limited the importance of hermeneutic enquiry. For Gadamer, to 'interpret means precisely to bring one's own preconceptions into play so that the text's meaning can really be made to speak for us.'[30] But he also raises a note of caution, indicating that an 'interpretation that was correct in itself would be a foolish ideal that mistook the nature of tradition. Every interpretation has to adapt itself to the hermeneutical situation to which it belongs.'[31] Hermeneutics, borne out of the work of Gadamer and more recently Ricoeur, involves the interpreter searching for meanings and understanding. In response to the criticisms of Gadamerian hermeneutics offered by Foucault and Habermas, Ricoeur's *Conflict of Interpretations* and the *Rule of Metaphor* leads to a form of textual hermeneutics which has traction because it helps to situate the researcher's own role and positionality alongside the way interpretation, dialogues, play occurs between text and context, and between rival interpretations which acts as a starting point for further interventions exploring narrative and meaning in particular conflicts.

Thus while a tension may remain between these two traditions, and for that matter the four philosophical approaches I have engaged with in this introduction, each provides a way into a critical reading of contemporary violence. That is to say, the aim of this book is to recognise these tensions but also move beyond them so as to engage with a programme of research which embraces the researcher's own role in the process of enquiry, while also highlighting the significance of dialogues within and between texts and horizons, within and between texts and contexts, and within and between rival interpretations.

In essence then, the application of hermeneutically inspired analysis to the study of war in Kosovo and Chechnya reveals that the phenomenon of war can be thought of as encompassing a multiplicity of discourses through which its meaning is produced. It is important to note here that I do not intend to provide a definitive conceptualisation of postmodern war, a fruitless task in any case. Rather, the purpose of this introductory chapter, and indeed this book as a whole, is to set out the bases and justifications for the engagement with what one might call a new conversation about contemporary violence. In this sense the conversation which this book engages with is part of the broader project of interpretive IR that seeks to move the boundaries beyond orthodox accounts of meaning,[32] but which is also linked to empirical methodologies such as social network analysis.

Conclusion: towards an interpretivist IR

The book itself does not rest on an idea of postmodern war. Instead, it offers a conversation informed by hermeneutics and narrative, discourses and interpretation. It strives to develop ideas stemming from the work on narratives and hermeneutics, so as to draw out a number of important aspects of violence in contemporary global politics, while informing and enriching debates concerned with epistemology, ontology and meaning. I argue that language and stories play an important role in IR and – through the application of inter-textual and contextual, as well as aesthetic and hermeneutic analysis – these stories inform what may be called an 'interpretive' or 'interpretivist' approach to global politics.[33] And while each of these terms can be used in particular ways and in specific contexts – especially when linked to historical and area studies or with an emphasis on local social networks – they provide a useful point of departure needed to re-introduce the study of war in IR.

Notes

1   T. Gurr, *Why Men Rebel* (Princeton, NJ: Princeton University Press, 1993); M. Kaldor, *New and Old Wars: Organized Violence in a New Era* (Cambridge: Polity Press, 1999); M. Duffield, *Global Governance and the New Wars: The Merger of Development and Security* (London: Zed Books, 2001).

2   E. Ringmar, *Identity, Interest and Action: A Cultural Explanation of Sweden's Intervention in the Thirty Year War* (Cambridge: Cambridge University Press, 1996); H. Suganami, 'Stories of War Origins: A Narrativist Perspective on the Causes of War', *Review of International Studies* Vol. 23, No. 4 (1997), pp. 401–418; H.Suganami, 'Explaining War: Some Critical Observations', *International Relations*, Vol. 16, No. 3 (2002), pp. 307–326.

3   W.B. Gallie, *Philosophers of War and Peace: Kant, Calusewitz, Marx, Engels and Tolstoy* (Cambridge: Cambridge University Press, 1989), p. 2.

4   C. Clausewitz, *On War* (Harmondsworth: Penguin, 1968).

5   I. Andrić, *The Bridge Over the Drina* (London: Harvill Press, 1994).

6   L. Tolstoy, *The Cossacks* (New York: Everyman's Library, 1994); L. Tolstoy, *War and Peace* (London: Penguin Classics, 2006).

7   H-G. Gadamer, *Philosophical Hermeneutics*, trans. D. Linge (Berkeley, CA: University of California Press, 1977), p. 29.

8   H-G. Gadamer, *Truth and Method* (London: Continuum, 2004); J. Caputo, *Radical Hermeneutics: Repetition, Deconstruction and the Hermeneutic Project* (Bloomington, IN: Indiana University Press, 1987); P. Ricoeur, *Hermeneutics and the Human Sciences: Essays on Language, Action and Interpretation*, trans. J.B. Thompson (Cambridge: Cambridge University Press, 2009); J. Grondin, *Introduction to Philosophical Hermeneutics* (London: Yale University Press, 1994).

9   J. Der Derian & M. Shapiro (eds.), *International/Intertextual Relations: Postmodern*

Readings of World Politics (Lexington, KY: Free Press, 1989); J. Weldes (ed.), *To Seek Out New Worlds: Exploring Links Between Science Fiction and World Politics* (Houndmills: Palgrave, 2003); S. Chan and P. Mandaville, 'Introduction: Within International Relations Itself, a New Culture Rises up', *The Zen of International Relations* (London: Palgrave, 2001), pp. 1–16.

10 H.G. Gadamer, *Truth and Method* (London: Continuum, 2004); P. Ricoeur, *The Conflict of Interpretations* (London: Continuum, 2004).

11 J. Baudrillard, 'From Symbolic Exchange and Death', in L.E. Cahoone (ed.), *From Modernism to Postmodernism: An Anthology* (Oxford and Malden, MA: Blackwell Publishers, 1996).

12 Ricoeur, *The Conflict of Interpretations*.

13 *Ibid.*; Ricouer, *Hermeneutics and the Human Sciences*.

14 W.V. Quine, *From A Logical Point Of View* (New York: Harper and Row, 1961), but even more H. Putnam, *Realism with a Human Face* (Cambridge, MA: Harvard University Press, 1990).

15 Z. Laïdi, 'The Delocalisation of Meaning', in P. Mandaville and A. Williams (eds.), *Meaning and International Relations* (London and New York: Routledge, 2003).

16 F. Jameson, 'Postmodernism or the Cultural Logic of Late Capitalism', *New Left Review*, No. 146 (1984), pp. 53–92; C. Coker, 'Post-Modernity and the End of the Cold War: Has War Been Disinvented?', *Review of International Studies*, Vol. 18, No. 2 (1992), pp. 189–198; C.H. Gray, *Postmodern War: The New Politics of Conflict* (New York: The Guilford Press, 1997); W.M.J. Olson, 'War Without a Center of Gravity: Reflections on Terrorism and Post-Modern War', *Small Wars & Insurgencies*, Vol. 18, No. 4 (2007), pp. 559–583.

17 P. Mandaville and A. Williams (eds.), *Meaning and International Relations* (London: Routledge, 2003). C. Moore and C. Farrands (eds.), *International Relations Theory and Philosophy* (London: Routledge, 2010).

18 M. Ignatieff, *Blood and Belonging: Journeys into the New Nationalism* (London: BBC Books, 1993); D. Turton (ed.), *War and Ethnicity: Global Connections and Local Violence* (Woodbridge: University of Rochester Press, 1997); P. Wallensteen and K. Axell, 'Armed Conflict at the End of the Cold War, 1989–92', *Journal of Peace Research*, Vol. 30, No. 3 (1993), pp. 331–346.

19 P. Neumann and M.L.R. Smith, *The Strategy of Terrorism: How it Works, and Why it Fails* (London: Routledge, 2008).

20 E. Husserl, *The Crisis of the European Sciences and Transcendental Phenomenology* (Evanston, IL: Northwestern University Press, 1970).

21 E. Husserl, *Logical Investigations* (London: Routledge, 1973).

22 A. Schutz, *The Phenomenology of the Social World*, trans. G. Walsh & F. Lehnert (Evanston, IL: Northwestern University Press, 1980 [1932]).

23 M. Merleau-Ponty, *Phenomenology of Perception* (London: Routledge, 2002).

24 A. Wendt, *Social Theory of International Politics* (Cambridge: Cambridge University Press, 1999), does recognise the influence of Schutz, unlike most constructivist writers in IR.

25 J-P. Sartre, *Being and Nothingness*, trans. H. Barnes (New York: Washington Square Press, 1992). Especially in this book, but the influence is evident throughout his work.

26 E. Levinas, *Totality and Infinity: An Essay on Exteriority*, trans. A. Lingis (Pittsburgh: Duquesne University Press, 1969).

27 D. Idhe, 'Editor's Introduction', in Ricoeur, *The Conflict of Interpretations*, p. xv.

28 *Ibid.*: p. xiv.

29 Gadamer, *Philosophical Hermeneutics*, p. 29.

30 Gadamer, *Truth and Method*, p. 398.

31 *Ibid.*

32 Moore and Farrands, *International Relations Theory and Philosophy*.

33 I am indebted to both Stephen Chan and Chris Farrands, who have both gone some way to outline what an interpretive approach to IR might look like. The ideas advanced here benefited from numerous conversations with both Stephen and Chris over a number of years.

1

Narrative identity and the challenge of literary global politics: towards interpretive pluralism

Some – if not all – contemporary wars are conducted for a multiplicity of reasons by an increasingly diverse set of actors. One corollary of this may be a reading of a broader spectrum of political violence which is neither exclusively political nor military, but is in part shaped by cultural and social forces captured in narrative. Even if narrative approaches have a long provenance in other disciplines, they have only recently touched the shores of IR. And yet, an approach which addresses accounts of narrative identity does much to capture the social, cultural and ontological assumptions which inform our interpretation of war.

This chapter stems from the recent contributions to theoretical debate by focusing on a turn in IR which is concerned with meaning, and which is tied into the real world relations of global politics through narratives.[1] The chapter begins by acknowledging the role of radical phenomenology as one root of interpretivism – which in turn has influenced narrative. The following sections address the theme of narrative identity, drawing on the work of Paul Ricoeur, before moving on to a discussion of founding events and storied culture. The final sections of the chapter draw these points together by engaging with the literary IR, thereby drawing attention to the challenge of reading literatures.

The roots of radical phenomenology

Although not intrinsic to the analysis which follows, one should also note that a trace can be made from the contemporary use of interpretive accounts of IR. These derive in part from the emergence of the existentialist school of thought which is itself a descendant of the phenomenology of Husserl and, more particularly, Heidegger. In this way, one can recognise that Jean

Paul Sartre, in the journal *Le Temps Moderne*, influenced Merleau-Ponty and Ricoeur. Others such as Gabriel Marcel and Albert Camus have developed phenomenology and existentialism in literary form. Elsewhere representatives of the Russian literary movement of the late nineteenth century also expressed a close affinity with existentialism and the ensuing philosophical interpretations of phenomena. In this sense, understanding the phenomenon of war derives from questioning the image and structures of social life, indicating the value of inter-subjective and reflective analysis. Nevertheless, phenomenological approaches to social relations, including those touched upon here in IR, face a set of questions about 'reality', which are at once profound and difficult.

Critical realists as well as orthodox positivists and realists would argue that postmodern analysis rooted in phenomenology does not have a position which adequately comes to terms with the 'real world'.[2] The response to the criticism that any phenomenological approach denies that there is any 'reality' to deal with, or alternatively, holds that if there is a reality phenomenological approaches (which subsume postmodern and poststructural approaches as subsets) are unable to grasp or identify it, is part of a broader argument.

Firstly, it must be recognised that this is not a straightforward either/or argument: there are many positions between the view that there is no reality at all and the view that there is a reality external to the human mind which empirical experience (and empirical experience alone) gains access to in such a way as to facilitate understanding, explanation and prediction. The latter view was so thoroughly demolished by Kant that it is a view few philosophers would defend, although it might be said to remain a 'common sense' view. Secondly, one might recognise the powerful criticisms of empiricism, but that those criticisms do not necessarily deny any possibility of knowledge of an external world. These criticisms in contemporary writing can be found in the work of, for example, Quine[3] and Putnam,[4] and in IR are reflected in much recent literature.[5] Thirdly, this leads to a conclusion that this work recognises that the external world does not only consist of text or discourse, although text and discourse are powerful and important elements of it (what might be called a soft or weak postmodern position).[6] It argues that the social world is constructed out of an interaction between individuals, networks, groups, language, and past experience.[7] A similar view is held by Ruggie, who identifies a specific class of institutional or social facts that comprise the world of global politics,[8] and Onuf.[9]

All this work reflects two core ideas. The first is that the ideas of the construction of social reality in which social analysts themselves take part, a key element of Schutz's analysis, which passes through to Giddens' understanding of social theory. Secondly, the idea that what the scholar of social relations is trying to get to grips with is not a physical or material world but a world of meanings, signifiers, significations and understandings, which are integrally (or internally, or logically) related to the actions which are based on them, in such a way that it is impossible to understand social action without understanding the varied meanings and ideas about meanings held by social agents. This leads, thirdly, to an important conclusion, one which has the effect of cutting out a large body of argument. If it is the social meanings and constructions held by agents that are important, especially in a particular context, we do not need to argue either way about whether there is an external reality in general. The question ceases to be important for this purpose, however much it may have a stranglehold on the philosophy of ontology in general. This position is similar to that held by Winch[10] in some respects, but it is not the same; it is not as apparently radical as Winch's claim, and it is not grounded in Wittgenstein's theory of language as his work is. Thus one reaches the satisfactory position that we can make an argument about meanings and signification, about the text of ideas and social constructions, without needing to support either the claim that 'that is all there is' (or 'there are turtles all the way down') or the contrary extreme view that there is a certainly knowable social reality analogous to the material world of an explanation in natural science. It is this moderate yet critical approach, which does not claim that the world is composed only of text or discourse, and which is suspicious of claims that there is a single fixed 'reality' without seeking to maintain that there is no reality at all, which consistently informs the analysis herein.

Hermeneutics is 'concerned with reconstructing the entire arc of operations by which practical experience provides itself with works, authors and readers'.[11] Hermeneutics then, captures the processes through which narrative identity is inscribed, through which fictional and historical stories, their production and reception, are apprehended and represented, and then subjects these processes to interpretation. Hermeneutics surrounds, and is embedded within, the production of narrative identity. For Ricoeur, 'hermeneutics is the theory of the operation of understanding in its relations to the interpretations of texts'.[12] Ricoeur develops this reading of phenomenological hermeneutics, noting how textual analysis draws out lived experience via the transmission of 'written documents, works, institutions, monuments, which make the historical past present to us'.[13] This leads to a series of concerns revolving around 'the problem of *multiple meaning*'[14] when interpreting texts. Ricoeur notes, for 'the interpreter, it is the text which has multiple meaning: the problem of multiple meaning is posed for him only if what is being considered is a whole in which events, persons, institutions, and natural or historical realities are articulated'.[15] The question is then, not just about the text and its interpretation – what Ricoeur labels 'textual hermeneutics' – but also about context. In order to explore this issue further, Ricoeur moves on to discuss the 'effect of context'.[16] He argues that the context 'plays the role of filter; when a single dimension of meaning passes through by means of play of affinities and reinforcements of other lexical terms, a meaning effect is created which can attain perfect univocity'.[17] The question, moving beyond textual hermeneutics, revolves around the way not only how texts are interpreted, but also how they are carried forward through stories. Narrativists note that stories can have a sequential order that connects 'events in a meaningful way for a definite audience, and thus offer insights about the world and/or people's experiences of it'.[18] But these mix, merge and blend with literary and historical genres, and shape slices of life.

But this is more than just a starting point: it helps to link work in the fields of hermeneutic, narrative and literary IR, precisely because it entertains questions about culturally inscribed narratives of identity.[19] It does so in at least two ways, first because narratives are themselves sensitive to the richness of work on ethnic connectedness and groupness, which moves beyond reading identity alone.[20] Second, the turn to different forms of narrative, be they fictional or historical, offers a space to integrate empirically driven work on social networks, which will be explored in the following chapters. Bearing these markers in mind, the plurality of the interpretive turn sets up a more detailed consideration of narrative developed in the work of Paul Ricoeur.

Narrative and identity

In the social and human sciences a plethora of writers draw on stories, narratives and narratology.[21] However, the various forms of narrative and narratology have arrived somewhat belatedly when turning to studies of identity in IR.[22] In IR, one of these writers, Hidemi Suganami, focuses on studies of war origins. Another, Erik Ringmar, turns to a narrative theory of action. And finally another, Iver Neumann, explores the applicability of narrative for studies of self and other relations. In various ways each has made a significant contribution to studies of narrative and identity, and yet each also suggests ways forward, opening up space for further analysis. For example Suganami identifies a need to read non-Western stories of 'war origins', while Iver Neumann's seminal work invites a critical constructivist reading of identity – which is not focused on the orthodoxy of IR: namely the nation-state. Neumann argues that studies of identity can be enhanced through the analysis of both those who hold state power as well as the 'competing stories of the self that exist as a constitutive element of a certain collective.'[23]

In order to build on this work, I seek here to draw on Paul Ricoeur's account of narrative. For narrativists, attempts to graft studies from the natural sciences onto the social sciences suppresses the variety of truth claims evident in culture. Narrative studies encourage the study of the plurality of stories which different cultures and communities, sub-groups and social networks tell about themselves. At least in part, narrative reacts to the dominant paradigm of rationality – and the related mechanistic reading of human behaviour – emphasising the significance of stories which help to create, refashion and portray forms of identity. In so doing, narrative draws attention to the richness of social phenomena linking judgements and actions – through webs of communication – to the social and cultural world. Narrative then, and more specifically both narrative identity and cultural narrative, provide a way to engage with the storied self. In so doing, this draws attention to context and location; act, purpose and agency; and the power of stories to apprehend memory, to re-inscribe identity, and to reproduce a sense of community.

Here, apart from the obvious attempt to demonstrate how fictional and historical narratives are interwoven, Ricoeur illustrates how narrative identity meditates between two different realms. He argues, 'reconfiguration makes this life itself a cloth woven of stories'.[24] This process of reconfiguration is reflexive, producing stories and accompanying symbols and tropes which are easy to recognise. Ricoeur states, 'an examined life is, in large part, one purged, one clarified by the cathartic effects of the narratives, be they historical or fictional, conveyed by our cultures'.[25] Narrative identity is self-reflexive and worked-upon by culture streamlining stories in a way that meditates between historical and fictional narratives. Indeed, 'the story of life comes to be constituted through a series of rectifications applied to previous narratives, just as the history of a people, or a collectivity, or an institution proceeds from the series of corrections that new historians bring to their predecessors' descriptions and explanations, and, step by step, to the legends that precede this genuine historiographical work'.[26] Inherent within the category of narrative identity is a process of refinement and exchange between history and fiction.

Ricoeur notes, the 'historical component of a narrative about oneself draws this narrative towards the side of chronicle submitted to the same documentary verifications as any other historical narration, while the fictional component draws it toward those imaginative variations that destabilize narrative identity'.[27] These conclusions lead Ricoeur to recognise that 'narrative identity continues to make and unmake itself', it 'thus becomes the name of a problem at least as much as it is that of a solution'.[28] Storied identity can be found in conversation between fictional and historical narratives which, arguably, can be used to supplement the critical constructivist account of self and other relations in IR.

The Ricoeurean account of narrative identity here, also serves to introduce a number of other themes which are worthy of attention. The first stems from a consideration of the temporal aspects of narrative. Ricoeur argues that '*time becomes human to the extent that it is articulated through a narrative mode, and a narrative attains its full meaning when it becomes a condition of temporal existence.*'[29] The second broad theme emanating from Ricoeurean narrative identity stems from his threefold account of mimesis. The first form of mimesis Ricoeur draws attention to is prefiguration. By prefiguration, Ricoeur means the practical field of life and action, 'its meaningful structures, its symbolic resources, its temporal character.'[30] This shapes narrative in a number of ways, particularly when linked to another aspect of mimesis, configuration. Configuration refers to emplotment, although this does not simply mean an ordering of events, but rather, 'opens up the kingdom of the *as if*.'[31] For Ricoeur, to 'follow a story is to move forward in the midst of contingencies and peripeteia under the guidance of an expectation that finds its fulfilment in the 'conclusion' of the story.'[32] Emplotment, or the act of configuration, grasps together the manifold aspects of time, helping to produce a storied account of identity. In *Oneself as Another*, he points out that narrative identity at the level of emplotment can 'be described in dynamic terms by the competition between a demand for concordance and the admission of discordances which, up to the close of the story, threaten this identity.'[33] Lastly, reconfiguration is the third aspect of mimesis which Ricoeur turns to. He notes, that this 'marks the intersection of the world of the text and the world of the hearer or reader: the intersection, therefore, of the world configured by the poem and the world wherein real action occurs and unfolds its specific temporality'.[34] In short, '*We are following therefore the destiny of a prefigured time that becomes a refigured time through the mediation of a configured time.*'[35]

According to Ricoeur, 'a story describes a sequence of actions, and experiences of a certain number of characters, whether real or imaginary. These characters are represented in situations which change or to the changes of which they react. These changes, in turn, reveal hidden aspects of the situation and the characters, giving rise to a new predicament which calls for thought or action or both.'[36] This leads to a consideration of 'the *development* of a plot and its correlate, the ability *to follow* a story'.[37] To follow a story 'is to understand the successive actions, thoughts and feelings as displaying a particular *directedness*'.[38] This leads to a consideration of the way stories are plotted and followed.

However it also leads to a threefold consideration of 'narrative time' so as to help understand how stories are directed and followed. For Ricoeur narrative time is constituted by: (1) time within which events take place (within-time-ness); (2) 'historicality' in which emphasis is placed on the past, and on the power of recovering and repetition; (3) and finally, plot. The first, 'within-time-ness', differs from 'linear time, even though it tends towards linearity due to its datable, public, and measurable nature and as a result of its dependence on points of reference in the world'.[39] Hence there is an ordinary, perhaps personal and public reading of time and events, leading to experience which has reference points in the world.

Secondly, Ricoeur recognises the role of historicality – 'that temporality consists in the deep *unity* of future, past, and present – or, rather, of coming forth, having been, and making present'.[40] Temporality is shaped by the 'stretching-along' of time – the unrelenting movement towards fate, towards a shared destiny – which Ricoeur calls 'being-toward-death'.[41] According to Ricoeur, this philosophical reading of finitude is given meaning through recollection and repetition; 'Through repetition, the character of time as stretching-along is rooted in the deep unity of time as future, past, and present, the backward move towards the past is retrieved in the anticipation of a project, and the endlessness of historical time is grafted on the finite structure of being-toward-death'.[42]

Finally, and most importantly here, narrative time is organised by plot. Plot is the

> intelligible whole that governs a succession of events in any story … A story is *made out of* events to the extent that plot *makes* events *into* a story. The plot, therefore, places us at a crossing point of temporality and narrativity: to be historical, an event must be more than a singular occurrence, a unique happening.[43]

Further analyses of these three aspects of narrative time are beyond the scope of this book. Nonetheless this brief interlude does serve to highlight the significance of a theory of narrative, how it ties together individual and collective stories which inform narrative identity.[44]

Narrative and founding events

According to Ricoeur, personal identity is linked to the constitution of narratives. Prompted by this notion of individual identity, Ricoeur notes that people also form collective identity through their conscious affiliation with a group.[45] Thus, 'the identity of a group, culture, people, or nation is not that of immutable substance, nor that of a fixed structure, but that, rather, of a recounted story.'[46] Group identities, however, are not the same as voluntary associations which can disappear and reappear, but are, instead, collective associations in which we are placed. The 'offshoot issuing from the union of history and fiction is the assignment to an individual or a community of a specific identity that we can call their narrative identity'.[47] Equally, for Ricoeur the notion of narrative identity 'can be applied to a community as well as an individual'.[48] So community and individual are constituted in 'their identity by taking up narratives that become for them their actual history'.[49]

In this way a collective history is produced, which may derive from private memory but is in itself distinctive, insofar as it generates narrative identity. Ricoeur notes that 'private and public memories are constituted simultaneously, according to the schema of mutual and reciprocal establishment'.[50] Particular events shape individual and collective identity. Atrocities, or indeed certain military campaigns, all tend to inscribe collective memory, and this is often reflected in the building of museums and statues, as well as the enactment of ceremonies and rituals designed to commemorate such events. In this way memorialisation occurs collectively, and is often borrowed from stories we learn from others, in groups, and is perhaps most often performed in rituals to those slain in battle or captured in lamentations to the dead.[51] Accordingly, 'our recollections are framed within collective narratives that are themselves reinforced by commemorations, that is, by public celebrations of outstanding events upon which the history of the groups to which we belong is dependent'.[52] This leads Ricoeur to examine what he calls founding events, which freeze history in certain ways, and which generate collective and sometimes national memories. Such founding events are repeated and (re)iterated, commemorated and celebrated, so as to become entrenched in culture. They are articulated through story, or as Ricoeur says, 'through its recitation, a story is incorporated into a community which it gathers together'.[53]

In *Memory, History and Forgetting*, Ricoeur notes that governing bodies draw on narratives to enhance legitimacy; 'stories of founding events, of glory and humiliation, feed the discourse of flattery or of fear'.[54] Indeed, 'forced memorization is thus enlisted in the service of the remembrance of those events belonging to the common history that are remarkable, even founding, with respect to the common identity. The circumspection of the narrative is thus placed in the service of the circumscription of the identity defining the community'.[55] Hence narratives shape and plot events into a chain which itself produces meaning for individuals, groups and communities or what may be called a 'formidable pact' between 'remembrance, memorization, and commemoration'.[56] In many ways then, the study of founding events helps to link actions and social phenomena to a broader concern with narrative embedded in culture.

To follow Ricoeur, we can identify a whole host of examples which may be considered as founding events, from the Field of the Black Crows in Kosovo, to the deportations of peoples from the North Caucasus in 1944.[57] For Ricoeur, 'as the characters of the narrative are emplotted at the same time the story is told, the narrative configuration contributes to modelling the identity of the protagonists of the action as it molds the contours of the action itself'.[58] In *Hermeneutics and the Human Sciences*, Ricoeur argues that the function of narrative is partly shaped through plot. He notes that 'a story describes a sequence of actions and experiences of a certain number of characters, whether real or imaginary. These characters are represented in situations which change or to the changes of which they react. These changes, in turn, reveal hidden aspects of the situation and the characters, giving rise to a new predicament which calls for thought or action or both. The response to this predicament brings the story to its conclusion'.[59] This is, in essence, the function of plot. But he goes on to note, beyond plot, that 'we are members of the field of historicity as storytellers, as novelists, as historians. *We belong to history before telling stories or writing history.* The game of telling is included in the reality told'.[60] If identity is tied to narrative, it would be reasonable to explore how particular stories gain purchase in the social and cultural worlds of different communities. And it is to this problem that we now turn, through an exploration of literary global politics.

The challenge of literary global politics

One of the first stumbling blocks one encounters when introducing literary readings of politics is the variety of texts upon which analyses can draw. Although both the aesthetic and hermeneutic are connected, the relationship between them requires a little introductory clarification. Indeed, as part of a preliminary consideration we must recognise that literature, as used throughout this book, does not stem from a coherent body of writing which has a distinctive form or a category which has a specific 'indisputable literary essence'.[61] Instead, the focus of the first chapter stems from the awareness of the literary as a way of conveying meanings. Literature and aesthetics as used throughout this book are employed to denote narrative forms or stories within a broader turn to interpretive IR theory.[62] But this does present a set of epistemological questions – how can we use such a range of sources or texts? And what relation does the study of literary global politics have with the recent turn to aesthetics and hermeneutics?

In order to answer these questions a little more detail is required. For the time being, the emphasis on narratives seeks to illustrate the complex relationship between interpretation and reception, and between the hermeneutic and aesthetic character of texts. Still further, selection is necessary when approaching such a vast body of literature and the choice of texts reflects a commitment to familiarity and intelligibility. In order to maintain consistency a detailed textual analysis of specific texts is not developed. But we can identify forms of meaning in the texts which are used. Understood in this light, the historical novel or Russian short story, the written account by a war correspondent, the human rights reports or highlander poetry all seek to capture meanings. They also seek to convey particular meanings through their different narrative structures. The historical novel or short story reflects a specific period in Russian literary development mirroring the emergence of Romanticism, Rationalism, political expansionism and the impact of the Enlightenment. More recently, accounts by war correspondents or human rights reports are linked to the emergence of Western modernity, whereas the Caucasian poetry seeks to challenge the colonial and cultural imperialism by apprehending oral histories of resistance as written texts.

Literary history figures as a distinctive type of culture. Through their work, Russian authors of the nineteenth and early twentieth centuries presented 'realism', factuality and educational information.[63] Beyond this, analysis of the literary history of a region reveals how texts operate with other texts. Thus, in reading literary history we can identify numerous contextual and dialogic practices which inform the processes of interpretation inside and outside narratives. Of course, narratives can be fact-oriented, empirical and observational in character. Yet literary texts are dialogic – they convey forms of knowledge – and are often linked to cultures, particular periods and specific encounters. Such narratives function through dialogue constituting a kind of compromise between forms of historical and empirical knowledge.

At the same time, they can also capture the psychological and cultural characteristics of identity which may – if analysed solely as political phenomenon – be otherwise categorised as irrational. In this way, the analysis of narratives offers insight into the cultural production of myth while also allowing analysis to draw upon the complex relationship between the author, the reader and responses to texts. In this study it would be erroneous to recognise conceptual boundaries between texts which are literary and sources which are neither designated as 'literature' nor simply categorised as non-literary. Instead, we shall approach these different narratives precisely because they offer insight into the relationship between culture, politics and identity – because the literary contains social, psychological, cultural and political 'stories' which have emerged through encounter.

Similarly, a number of caveats must be presented in order to defend the usage of a diverse range of sources such as literature and art. Nevertheless, stories of violence cannot be understood effectively without taking the artistic as an important point of departure. The argument becomes, in a very general sense, that literature allows insight into the transformation of violence from the Western discourse of progressive, technologised and material warfare – to violence which is not stripped of its narrative features. Here, we may turn to the work of novelist and literary critic Milan Kundera in order to expose the role that literature and the novel may play in expressing forms of being. The novel is born of critical ontology because 'through its own logic the novel discovered the various dimensions of existence one by one'.[64] Still further, 'the novelist is neither historian nor prophet: he is an explorer of existence'.[65] The novel is a means of expressing 'being' and is subjectivity grounded in what Kundera calls 'polyhistoricism'. Thus, instead of disjuncture of the modern condition, the novel presents 'one current event among many, a gesture with no tomorrow'.[66] The effort, then, is to interpret the radical creativity of writing through the writer and through its cultural reception. When taken together, it is clear that analysis cannot investigate political puzzles without reference to literature because it captures the 'spirit of complexity and continuity'. Evidently, it is stories – myths and legends – that evoke agency and it is the manifold forms of literature that operate as a vehicle for expressing agency. In this way, the characterisation of violence is inscribed culturally through intersubjective meaning within ontology or as part of 'being'. But, of course, approaching violence and war hermeneutically establishes identity as a site of constant contestation played out through representations in culture, in symbols or rituals, and organised through the evocation of transcultural meaning. In this manner, as Chan has demonstrated, hermeneutic analysis may not only draw on texts, which means 'that a silent and illiterate discourse of understandings and intuition is possible'.[67] Thus, the radical creativity of writing can be supplemented by interpreting how global politics appears to the reader.

Telling stories offers insight into the dialogues of encounter between the past and present because 'the novel cannot live in peace with the spirit of our time'.[68] As Kundera illustrates, the novel may offer insight beyond causality because it 'brings to light the causeless, incalculable, even mysterious aspect of human action'.[69] The term literature is used here to cover three particular means of expressing meaning – the novelistic story, Russian and Caucasian poetry and journalistic accounts. The reason for this emphasis is rather simple since each is an expression of encounter and may be linked to particular facets of the Chechen wars. In the twentieth century, it is these three forms which inscribed cultural life and function to express particular dimensions of Russo-Chechen relations.

In particular, war presents political puzzles. These may be constituted through acts or what may be called transgressions in the face of violence

– such as atrocity or solidarity – which contradict the normalcy of political discourses. By drawing on literature, analysis of such events offers insight into the taboos of killing, illustrating how 'intimate acts of violence' are 'imbued with language, emotion and desire'.[70] The key, then, is to identify the complex forces which condition contemporary violence, and interpreting the evocative dimensions of global politics through literature 'provides key insights into these inaudible political spheres'.[71] In essence, by employing literature, IR theory may be able to relate to the different referents that condition violence including the courage, shame, cruelty and honour commonly associated with stories of war.[72] In this way, writers, and more recently journalists, characterise violence through stories.

These stories may, on the one hand, relate to transnational expressions of identity such as tragedy, and, on the other, may be culturally specific and relate to the commemoration of death through folkloric tales.[73] A network of metaphor and genre, closely associated with literature and literary criticism is therefore brought into focus as a way of reading global politics.[74] At this point we should retrace some of the issues related to the relationship between literature and global politics.

Literature and global politics

The contributions to forms of knowledge made by literature have often been interrogated by philosophers and political scientists alike. Here, however, a further set of questions arises: how is literature received, understood and interpreted? In fact, the way texts are 'encountered' and 'interpreted' has long been a central concern of literary criticism. Literary criticism has itself drawn upon the possibilities of interpretations and the problems of authorship.[75] This work has established that meanings and interpretations occur in the production and reception of texts. It is the interrogation of the reception of texts, of reception theory, which literature exposes in reading the 'political'. In *Popular Dissent, Human Agency and Global Politics*, Roland Bleiker notes that 'a text takes off in multiple directions and becomes an object of appropriation over which the author invariably loses control'.[76] As Bleiker notes, it is through the understanding of texts, through interpreting their aesthetic quality, which may enable us to understand political puzzles in a different light. In absorbing meanings, a text is inscribed by and, therefore, becomes part of its own meaning. Therefore literary texts represent an 'aesthetic horizon' offering insight into the contingencies of subjectivity and being. This horizon captures expectations and prejudices which shift and change. Rather than positing a one-dimensional ontology, this approach draws on literature, which itself stems from the reflexivity associated with multiple ontologies.

As Suganami has illustrated, the most obvious advantage of using stories to explore global politics stems from the capacity of literature to highlight the otherwise unnoticed multiplicities of agency. As a further contribution to Suganami's narrative IR theory, we may see aesthetic IR as a way of unsettling the dominant political discourses of war by highlighting the role of agency. Thus, the 'aesthetic turn' in IR theory has a further major consequence for the analysis of identities. At first sight the consequence seems somewhat clear. Identities are, in many cases, inter-subjectively grounded and played out in culture. In this way, discourses of identity may not only be seen as partly de-territorialised but also constantly reconstituted through the cultural interplay of violence. Thus, not only identity but also violence which stems from identity may, to some degree, always be in the act of becoming. While this is too big an issue to go into in any detail here, the effect, when combined with technological innovations, has been to subvert the privileged political concept of war.

The confluence of such forces often results in a distinctive form of violence such as the use of kidnapping or suicide attacks, which will be explored in more detail later in the book. More broadly we can see that features, such as the phenomenon of foreign fighters, are comparable and yet rather elusive when considered against other comparable conflicts. This indicates that it is the experience of violence which inscribes its meaning and which is born out in 'telling stories of war'. As the war correspondent Anthony Loyd emphasises: 'the scale of violence, fear and horror, it left anything in my experience so far behind as to make it almost insignificant'.[77] Still further, he highlights that analysis 'can grade conflicts according to intensity: low, medium and high'.[78] Yet 'Chechnya blew the bell off the end of the gauge, and revealed an extreme of war to me that I had no conception of. Afterwards my understanding of conflict was never quite the same again. It was indeed a glimpse from the edge of hell'.[79] Unfortunately, it appears that the case of Chechnya provides a set of different stories of war which themselves stem from 'other knowledges'. The literary contribution here is twofold; it explores the nature of violence born of 'other' knowledge and experience and is part of a process of relaying this vision of violence across cultures. This body of literature 'can be of much help because it has long been engaged in cross-cultural conversation'.[80] But in any case, because they are grounded in 'movement and dialogues', such cross-cultural conversations traverse political boundaries. Indeed, it is not uncommon to hear reporters and participants talk about the sheer brutality of different conflicts in order better to explain their character. In a general sense, through literature and storytelling, analysis can draw on the imaginative and factual dimensions of literature better to understand violence *in extremis*.

Conclusion

This chapter has demonstrated a number of interrelated interventions: first, the radical phenomenological heritage which shapes hermeneutic analysis and readings of narrative adopted by Paul Ricoeur which can be used to explore the examples of contemporary violence in Kosovo and Chechnya; second, correspondingly, that this work can be bolstered by hermeneutic interventions beyond the commonly-held post-positivism of the late 1990s, through a reading of narrative and founding event; third, that cultural narratives expose IR to the plurality of agency, social networks and historical accounts of global politics; finally, that literary global politics and literatures provides a useful body of work which may be used to draw together intertext and context. These four theoretical points might broadly be considered as insightful ways to read the conflicts in the Balkans and Caucasus drawing on area studies and social network analysis.

Notes

1   P. Mandaville and A. Williams (eds.), *Meaning and International Relations* (London: Routledge, 2003); S. Chan and P. Mandaville, 'Introduction: Within International Relations Itself, a New Culture Rises up', *The Zen of International Relations* (London: Palgrave, 2001), pp. 1–16.

2   H. Patomäki and C. Wright, 'After Postpositivism? The Promises of Critical Realism', *International Studies Quarterly*, Vol. 44, No. 2 (2000), pp. 213–237.

3   W.V. Quine, *From A Logical Point Of View* (New York: Harper and Row, 1961).

4   H. Putnam, *Realism with a Human Face* (Cambridge, MA: Harvard University Press, 1990).

5   K. Booth and S. Smith (eds.), *International Relations Theory Today* (Philadelphia, PA: University of Pennsylvania Press, 1995).

6   P. Rosenau, *Post-Modernism and the Social Sciences: Insights, Inroads and Intrusion* (Princeton, NJ: Princeton University Press, 1992).

7   See especially, Putnam, *Realism With a Human Face*.

8   J.G. Ruggie, *Constructing the World Polity: Essays on International Political Theory* (London: Routledge, 1998).

9   N.G. Onuf, *World of Our Making: Rules and Rule in Social Theory and International Relations* (Columbia, SC: University of South Carolina Press, 1989).

10 P. Winch, *The Idea of a Social Science and Its Relation to Philosophy* (London: Routledge & Kegan Paul, 1958).

11 P. Ricoeur, *Time and Narrative: Volume One* (Chicago: University of Chicago Press, 1990), p. 53.

12 P. Ricoeur, 'the Task of Hermeneutics', *Philosophy Today*, Vol. 17, No. 2 (1973), p. 112.

13 P. Ricoeur, 'Phenomenology and Hermeneutics', *Noûs*, Vol. 9, No. 1 (1975), p. 97.

14 Paul Ricoeur, *The Conflict of Interpretations* (London: Continuum, 2004), p. 62.

15 *Ibid.*, p. 63.

16 *Ibid.*, p. 69.

17 *Ibid.*

18 L. Hinchman and S. Hinchman (eds.), *Memory, Identity, Community: The Idea of Narrative in the Human Sciences* (Albany, NY: State University of New York Press, 1997), p. xvi.

19 K. Tololyan, 'Narrative Culture and the Motivation of the Terrorist', in J. Shotter and K.J. Gergen (eds.), *Texts of Identity* (London: Sage, 1998), pp. 99–118.

20 R. Brubaker, *Ethnicity Without Groups* (Cambridge, MA: Harvard University Press, 2004).

21 The human sciences are replete with studies of narrative and narratology. Some of the most well-known accounts can be found in the work of Vladimir Propp, Gérard Genette, and more recently Hayden White. For example, see G. Genette, *Narrative Discourse: An Essay in Method* (New York: Cornell University Press, 1995).

22 H. Suganami, 'Western (?) Stories of War Origins', in S. Chan, P. Mandaville and R. Bleiker (eds.), *The Zen of International Relations: IR Theory From East to West* (Houndmills: Palgrave, 2001), pp. 17–36; E. Ringmar, *Identity, Interest and Action: A Cultural Explanation of Sweden's Intervention in the Thirty Year War* (Cambridge: Cambridge University Press, 1996); I. Neumann, *Uses of the Other: 'The East' in European Identity Formation* (Minneapolis, MN: University of Minnesota Press, 1999). Outside of IR the political geographer, David Campbell also touches on narrative accounts of identity, making theoretical capital out of the use of Hayden White's work. In doing so, Campbell offers a gripping theoretical account of deconstruction. See D. Campbell, *Writing Security: United States Foreign Policy and the Politics of Identity* (Manchester: Manchester University Press, 1998); D. Campbell, *National Deconstruction: Violence, Identity, and Justice in Bosnia* (Minneapolis, MN: University of Minnesota Press, 1998).

23 Neumann, *Uses of the Other*, p. 224.

24 P. Ricoeur, *Time and Narrative: Volume Three* (Chicago: University of Chicago Press, 1988), p. 246.

25 *Ibid.*, p. 247.

26 *Ibid.*

27 *Ibid.*, pp. 248–249.

28 *Ibid.*, p. 249.

29 Ricoeur, *Time and Narrative: Volume One*, p. 52. Italics here, and in all quoted text throughout this book, indicate original emphasis.

30 *Ibid.*, p. 54.

31 *Ibid.*, p. 64.

32 *Ibid.*, p. 66.

33 P. Ricoeur, *Oneself as Another* (Chicago: University of Chicago Press, 1994), p. 140.

34 Ricoeur, *Time and Narrative: Volume One*, p. 571.

35 *Ibid.*, p. 54.
36 P. Ricoeur, *Hermeneutics and the Human Sciences* (Cambridge: Cambridge University Press, 2009), p. 277.
37 P. Ricoeur, 'Narrative Time', *Critical Inquiry*, Vol. 7, No. 1 (1980), p. 172.
38 Ricoeur, *Hermeneutics and the Human Sciences*, p. 277.
39 Ricoeur, 'Narrative Time', p. 170.
40 *Ibid.*, pp. 180–181.
41 *Ibid.*, p. 180.
42 *Ibid.*, p. 182.
43 *Ibid.*, p. 171.
44 For more on the links between narrative and narratology drawing on the work of Ricoeur see S. Chan, 'A Problem for IR: How shall we Narrate the Saga of Bestial Man', *Global Society*, Vol. 17, No. 4 (2003), pp. 385– 413.
45 K. Fierke, 'Whereof We Can Speak, Thereof We Must Not Be Silent: Trauma, Political Solipsism and War', *Review of International Studies*, Vol. 30, No. 4 (2004), pp. 471–491.
46 P. Ricoeur, 'Reflections on a New Ethos for Europe', *Philosophy and Social Criticism*, Vol. 21, No. 5/6 (1995), p. 5.
47 P. Ricoeur, *Time and Narrative: Volume Three* (Chicago: University of Chicago Press, 1988), p. 246.
48 *Ibid.*, p. 247.
49 *Ibid.*
50 P. Ricoeur, 'Entre mémoire et histoire', cited in Bernard Bauenhauer, *Paul Ricoeur: The Promise and Risk of Politics* (Oxford: Rowman & Littlefield Publishers, 1998), p. 129.
51 In keeping with the theme of Chechnya throughout this book, see the story of Yevgeny Rodionov whose grave is a site for pilgrims from across Russia. Andrew Osborn, 'How a young conscript became a Russian Saint', *The Independent*, 24 November 2004.
52 Ricoeur, 'Entre mémoire et histoire', p. 129.
53 Ricoeur, 'Narrative Time', p. 176.
54 P. Ricoeur, *Memory, History, Forgetting* (Chicago: University of Chicago Press, 2006), p. 85.
55 *Ibid.*, p. 85.
56 *Ibid.*
57 J. Mertus, *Kosovo: How Myths and Truths Started a War* (London: University of California Press, 1999); B.G. Williams, 'Commemorating "The Deportation" in Post-Soviet Chechnya: The Role of Memorialization and Collective Memory in the 1994–1996 and 1999–2000 Russo-Chechen Wars', *History & Memory*, Vol. 1, No. 12 (2000), pp. 101–134.
58 Ricoeur, *Memory, History, Forgetting*, p. 85.
59 P. Ricoeur, 'The Narrative Function', *Hermeneutics and the Human Sciences*, p. 277.
60 *Ibid.*, p. 294.
61 For a detailed analysis of the differences between the functions of literature, see T. Bennett, 'Criticism and Literature', in *Formalism and Marxism* (Methuen: London

and New York, 1979), pp. 3–17.

62 For a useful discussion of the role of literature and narrative in political theory, see J. Horton and A. Baumeister (eds.), *Literature and the Political Imagination* (London: Routledge, 1996).

63 S. Layton, 'Introduction', in *Russian Literature and Empire: Conquest of the Caucasus from Pushkin to Tolstoy* (Cambridge: Cambridge University Press, 1994), p. 12.

64 M. Kundera, *The Art of Novel* (Chatham: Gallimard, 1990), p. 5.

65 *Ibid.*, p. 44.

66 *Ibid.*, p. 19.

67 S. Chan, 'Writing Sacral IR: An Excavation Involving Kung, Eliade and Illiterate Buddhism', *Millennium: Journal of International Studies*, Vol. 29, No. 3 (2000), p. 579.

68 Kundera, *The Art of Novel*, p. 19.

69 *Ibid.*, p. 57.

70 J. Bourke, *An Intimate History of Killing: Face to Face Killing in 20th Century Warfare* (London: Granta, 1999), p. 12.

71 R. Bleiker, 'Learning from Art: A Reply to Holden's "World Literature and World Politics"', *Global Society*, Vol. 17, No. 4 (2003), p. 419.

72 L. Tolstoy, *The Raid and Other Stories* (Oxford: Oxford University Press, 1988), p. 25.

73 For the former, see A. Politkovskaya, *A Dirty War: A Russian Reporter in Chechnya* (London: Harvill Press, 2001), p. 56, and for the latter, see J. Colausso, *Nart Sagas from the Caucasus: Myths and Legends from the Circassians, Abazas, Abkhaz, and Ubykhs* (Oxford: Princeton University Press, 2002).

74 M. Moriarty, *Roland Barthes* (Stanford: Stanford University Press, 1991), pp. 59–72. Within IR theory, a good example of using genre to read global politics can be found in the work of Louiza Odysseos; see, for instance, 'Laughing Matters: Peace, Democracy and the Challenge of the Comic Narrative', *Millennium: Journal of International Studies*, Vol. 30, No. 3 (2001), pp. 709–732.

75 See, for instance, Hans Jauss and his work on 'reception theory'. See also Michael Moriarty, *Roland Barthes*, pp. 31–43, 91–102.

76 R. Bleiker, *Popular Dissent, Human Agency and Global Politics* (Cambridge: Cambridge University Press, 2000), p. 65.

77 A. Loyd, *My War Gone By, I Miss it So* (London: Transworld Publishers, 2000), pp. 235–236.

78 *Ibid.*, p. 236.

79 *Ibid.*

80 Bleiker, 'Learning from Art', p. 427.

2

Kosovo and Chechnya/Kosova and Ichkeria

This chapter will introduce Kosovo and Chechnya as examples of contemporary conflict. Delving into the history and geopolitics of Kosovo and Chechnya will help, insofar as it draws attention to a range of features, as well as a range of similar and dissimilar trends which inscribed the character of violence. These trends and features may be discernible in mythic stories of war and identity. In this way, analysis of geopolitical legacies and historical narratives provides valuable and often neglected insight into both regions. The analysis which follows draws on the account of storied identity, cultural narratives and founding events in Chapter 1 – locating Kosova and Ichkeria in what may be called a much broader historically conditioned narrative space. It does so precisely because the milieu of earlier periods in which empires emerged and declined, and in which ideologies flourished and crumbled – particularly in the Cold War and post-Soviet period – shaped the political agendas of the anti-Russian Chechen armed resistance movement and the anti-Serb Kosova Liberation Army.

Myth and the emergence of narrative identity

Hidemi Suganami has persuasively argued that narratives can be used to bridge the divide between structure and agency, precisely because the social world – including material and non-material aspects of it – can 'be seen as a gigantic river of innumerable stories about itself and its components, which are mutually reinforcing, partially overlapping, incompatible, or incommensurate, continuously told, retold, modified, rejected or forgotten'.[1] Stories are therefore told, and retold, perhaps in the form of myths, providing a constitutive part of collective narratives of identity. When considering the mythic character of war, the journalist Chris Hedges notes that we often 'imbue events with meanings they do not have. We see defeats as signposts on the road to ultimate victory. We demonize the enemy so that our opponent is no longer human. We view ourselves, our people, as the embodiment of absolute goodness.'[2] He goes on to note that the 'potency of myth is that it allows us to make sense of the mayhem of violent death … It allows us to believe that we have achieved our place in human society because of a long chain of heroic endeavours … By turning history into myth we transform random events into a chain of events directed by a will greater than our own, one that is determined and preordained.'[3]

Meanwhile George Schöpflin has offered a compelling account of the importance of myth, particularly when turning to nationalism. For Schöpflin, myth 'is one of the ways in which collectivities – in this context, more especially nations – establish and determine the foundations of their own being, their own systems of morality and values. In this sense, therefore, myth is a set of beliefs, usually put forth as a narrative, held by a community about itself'.[4] He goes on to note that 'nations are partly held together by their myths of identity, origins, future or other experiences'.[5] Thus myths are storied. As they are told and retold they establish boundaries within communities. For Schöpflin,

> myths contribute to the creation of identity by establishing the boundaries of identity, by binding together members of the nation, by excluding non-members through collective meanings by which individuals know themselves and their fellow members, recognising without further reflection the tacit limits of solidarity, obligation and trust and pursing transactions with a minimum of negotiation.[6]

Significantly then, the study of myths provides an interpretive reservoir which narrative and identity claims draw upon. In other words, myth provides a function when turning to collective identities, precisely because it produces

> an intellectual and cognitive monopoly in that it seeks to establish the sole way of ordering the world and defining world views. For the community to exist as a community, this monopoly is vital, and the individual members of that community must broadly accept the myth. Note here that myth is not identical with falsehood or deception. Members of a community may be aware that the myth they accept is not strictly accurate, but because myth is not history, this does matter.[7]

It is in essence the content and function of myth, not the historical accuracy of the story which is of interest. Myths, for Schöpflin, have a number of functions, namely: they enable and act as an instrument for self-definition; myths allow for the transfer of identity – thus enabling a new identity to be superimposed onto an older identity; they are communicative, both for the creation of, and the maintenance of the illusion of community; myths define cognitive fields – or ways of understanding communities and groups – thereby functioning to simplify the complexity of identity claims; they support, reinforce and are deployed by political elites, often giving those elites legitimacy; they provide a powerful explanatory device for the fate of communities; they maintain, filter and screen memory – creating, stigmatising and holding irrational beliefs about mythic enemies; and they often function as a component of culture.[8] Hence stories become entwined with myths and together they help to create individual and collective boundaries. The key then becomes the establishment of a coherent myth, one that is reproducible, legible and digestible. This in turn, leads to a consideration of

> myth, ritual and symbol. In simple terms, myth is the narrative, the set of ideas, whereas ritual is the acting out, the articulation of myth; symbols are the building blocks of myth and the acceptance and veneration of symbols is a significant aspect of rituals … Thus myths are encoded in rituals, liturgies and symbols, and reference to a symbol can be quite sufficient to recall the myth for members of the community without need to return to the ritual … Members of a community of shared symbols can continue to recognize one another and maintain communication even after they have abandoned their language (in the philological sense). The relationship between grammatical language and symbolic language is a continuous one; each sustains the other.[9]

In this way rituals and specific symbols serve to produce collective identities. In the case of post-Communist Russia and Serbia, the symbolism of religion became entwined in the re-articulation of a shared sense of collective or national identity. In a sense then, as this chapter argues, the wars in Kosovo and Chechnya were not about religion per se, but rather about maintaining and iterating a coherent sense of national identity – Serbia and Russia became protectors against invaders (Turks, Muslims, Arabs). The inception of the Serbian administration under the leadership of Slobodan Milosevič drew on ritual and symbols associated with the Church, while in Russia the Putin administration made similar, although more implicit usage of religious and national symbols. At the same time, the armed resistance movements in the Balkans and Caucasus sought to deploy symbols of national identity, establishing a mythic link to particular territories – in Kosovo a flag containing a twin-headed eagle, or the Ichkerian flag containing a wolf – were used to tie their sense of collective identity with nature, thereby establishing a sense of identity which differentiated them from what were considered to be occupying forces. Interestingly, over time the Chechen use of symbols would change, as internal radicalisation impacted upon the resistance movement.

The previous chapter began by drawing on an account of imaginative or fictional stories which inform the social and cultural theories of narrative identity. If myths and symbols inform a sense of collective identity, identity claims also need to be contextualised historically. Here then, it is important to turn to the historical legacies – the complex mix of the past – in cultural, personal and perhaps even journalistic stories which, when woven together, offer insight or give practices a sense of meaningfulness. In part historical narrative may be tied to myth and legend, ritual and ceremony, literature and reportage. For example, it may be said that the Russian short story gives insight into the cultural specificity of identity formation in both Russian and Caucasian highlander poetry and provides a further expression of this process of encounter.[10] At the same time, the novel or short story examines the role that myth from the remote past plays in controlling our present. We can see here how some literature may serve to identify the emergence of a modern Russia and how the recent Russian campaigns are conditioned by past events as emphasised by Gholam-Reza Sabri-Tabrizi:

> Voronstov's insistence on the destruction of the village can be attributed first and foremost to the fact that he came to view the battle as a fight for his honour, a question of prestige and a challenge to Mother Russia. It is worth noting that the recent policy of the Russian state towards Chechnya is similar to that of tsarist Russia in this respect.[11]

Although the emphasis in Sabri-Tabrizi's commentary is on the first Russo-Chechen campaign it is evident that the mythic image of the Russian hero has, again, had an impact upon the representation and practice of war fighting in the second campaign. The representational myth and storytelling function of global politics has served to produce and reinforce the imaginary continuation of Russian policy in the Caucasus.[12]

In other words, throughout *Hadji Murat*, *The Raid* and *Prisoner in the Caucasus* distinctive characteristics of Russian and Caucasian highlander identity come to the fore. By employing fiction as a means of representing these characteristics, the short story and the folklore tale provide a way into interpreting culturally specific forms of identity. Similarly in Serbia – and more generally in many oral Slavic traditions – professional singers were viewed as traditional public storytellers, recounting heroic deeds and evoking history. These heroic songs formed the basis of what would later become epic poems known as *bugarshtitse*. This feudal form of Serbo-Croat epic poetry sought to reflect on the need for 'brotherly love which transcends fratricide and expresses moral needs beyond the actualities of social custom and history'.[13]

Equally as the historian Noel Malcolm writes in *Kosovo: A Short History*, the region is

> one of the cultural crossing-places of Europe: it was probably central to the survival of the Albanian language and to the development of the Romanian one: it

became the geographical heart of an important medieval kingdom; it was one of the most characteristic parts of the Ottoman Empire in Europe; and it was the area in which the modern Albanian national movement was born, and had its greatest successes and failures.[14]

All this invites a reading of the stories of Russo-Chechen and Serbian and Kosovar violence, a point raised in Chapter 1. In a way literature, the short story or poem – the oral histories of Serbia and Albania – offer a way to link the past with the present precisely because they are reflections on the interface between myth and experience. In both cases inter-ethnic tensions and cultural differences were exacerbated by mythological readings of identity offering a further theme through which to (re)view accounts of contemporary conflict. In effect, both cases were storied. These stories were tied to the very geography of each region. In parts of Kosovo, particularly the mountainous areas of neighbouring Macedonia and Albania, state attempts by the Serbian authorities to assert control over the Kosovar peoples was problematic, even when aided by the support of neighbouring Slavic nations. Similarly in Chechnya, the mountainous regions to the south meant the geography was ripe for a protracted form of guerrilla war.

In effect then, the spatial entities of Kosovo and Chechnya, their names (locally they are referred to as Kosova and Ichkeria respectively) and locations on the borders of crumbling empires, as well the cultural influence of Ottoman, Persian and Pan-Slavism created the political space in which new myths could emerge and in which narratives of national identity gained a foothold. As we will see in Chapter 3, in recent years this process of identity re-articulation drew on the deep-seated ideas of resistance to foreign occupation, coupled with attempts to refashion a sense of post-Communist belonging and identity. But such interventions may only take us so far, in that they do not link the role of various local groups or regional political forces with broader historical narratives.

Kosovo/Kosova

Until recent years Kosovo was a province of the post-Dayton Serbian Republic. As a region it borders Montenegro, Albania and Macedonia, hosting a population of around one and a half million people. The inhabitants come from a rich array of ethnic, political and religious backgrounds. In Bosnia, the Serbs, Croats and Muslims spoke similar languages, making religion the marker of difference. Yet in Kosovo, Albanians, Serbs, Turks and Gypsies all speak different languages, while there is a threefold religious divide into Catholics, Muslims, including a substantial number of Shi'a dervish orders, as well as Orthodox Serbs. Therefore Kosovo was essentially a 'pluralistic society'.[15]

Throughout history, Kosovo itself has been named and renamed by these different groups, assimilating the ways of conquering armies and leading to the mass migrations of peoples into and out of Kosovo proper. Kosovo has, somewhat obviously, been the site of numerous conflicts.[16] More often than not, violence in the region has revolved around the complexities of family and clan rivalries. As Ger Duijzings writes, since living conditions in Kosovo were both harsh and highly competitive, the extended family provided 'not only a kind of safety net (as is the case in Western Europe), but also a major source of group solidarity and primary defensive-and-attack unit, strictly organised along corporate and patriarchal lines'.[17] Indeed Albanian Kosovar identity drew on a

> strong fixation on the family or lineage; distrust towards those who are not one's kin; a strong pressure to protect the family's integrity and avenge infringements upon its reputation ... [which means that] loyalties beyond one's own family are highly unstable, changeable and fluid.[18]

One particular feature of this type of 'atomised social life' was the blood feud, which, as Miranda Vickers notes, was only halted as a result of the decision to resist Serbian attacks in the latter part of the 1990s.

The Battle of Kosovo: The Field of the Black Crows

It is perhaps the Battle of Kosovo which has shaped much of the legend and myth about Serbian relations with Kosovo, and the respective claims to the region.[19] The battle took place in 1389 when, according to legend, the Serbian Prince Lazar led a band of knights against Turkish invaders led by Sultan Murad. The recovery of a heroic legend – replete with examples of generosity by the mythic Serbian Prince – were immortalised in songs and poetry. According to Peter Levi, Kosovo became the focal point in the story of the fall of the Serbian empire. He writes, to 'generations it was like the fall of Troy, intensely and personally felt ... They thought the death of Lazar and his lords was a heroic choice, a kind of martyrdom'.[20] On the one hand, the epic poem helped to establish an image of Serbian martyrdom, while, on the other hand, the Battle of Kosovo was viewed as a turning point in Serb history, the end of Serbian independence. Although never becoming compiled in a full-length epic, the fragments and versions of the myth remained powerful tools for mobilising a sense of Serbian narrative identity which – coupled with the idea of resurrection – was to re-emerge in the late 1980s.

For the historian Noel Malcolm, the Battle of Kosovo was much more complex than that depicted in Serbian legend. Instead, Malcolm argues that

Serbs and other Christians fought alongside the Turkish Muslims at the battle which, although not uncommon in feudal times, alters the heroic narrative which simply compartmentalises Serbian, Christian 'us', and Turkish, Muslim 'other'. Malcolm writes how the story of the Battle of Kosovo became 'a totem or talisman of Serbian identity, so that this event has a status unlike anything else in the history of the Serbs. To call this ideologically charged story the "myth of Kosovo" is not to suggest that everything in it is false, but rather to indicate the talismanic way in which it operates.'[21] In fact, as Malcolm argues, the Battle of Kosovo was not the Turkish victory which destroyed the medieval Serbian empire: Serbian statehood survived for some years after the battle, while, according to other historians, it was probably the battle at Marcia in Bulgaria in 1371 that 'opened the way to the overall Ottoman conquest of the Balkans'.[22]

Nonetheless, the Battle of Kosovo also serves to demonstrate how a tragic Serbian narrative emerged, tainted with religious meaning. The story, according to Serb historians, traces the life and downfall of an individual as a tragedy. The tragedy acts as a vehicle with the Serbian protagonist representing the Prince as a man capable of superhuman acts of generosity and nobility, who suffered, was betrayed by Vuk Brankovic, and who was ultimately sacrificed at Kosovo. The mythic story acts then as an allegory for the Serbian people whose independence was lost at the Battle of Kosovo.

However, the battle was not a complete victory for the Ottoman Turks, but part of a slow process of empire building. It was only after the fall of Constantinople in 1455 that the Ottomans eventually captured Serbia proper. Moreover, the ensuing years of Ottoman rule also provided for the integration of peoples from the Balkans into the Turkish empire, and indeed, coexistence between Christians and Muslims in one form or another (in many cases Christian princes converted to Islam, and rose to prominent positions in the state).[23]

Kosovo and the decline of the Ottoman Empire

Once again, when turning to a consideration of the decline of the Ottoman Empire the idea of an allegorical tale comes to the fore as great power politics, internal migrations and religious differences generated tensions between the peoples of the Balkans. By the seventeenth century, as the academic and writer Miranda Vickers notes, a considerable portion of the Serbian Christian population migrated from Kosovo, as the Austro-Ottoman wars gathered pace. Fearing the threat of reprisals from the Sublime Porte (the traditional name of the Ottoman government which originally derived from French, and means the imperial gate or seat of government in Turkey), a massive social upheaval took place. Unable to fight Ottomans, the greater part of the inland Serbian population accepted ... an offer of asylum in the Habsburg territories. In 1690, therefore, 37,000 Serbian families from the Kosovo region, under the leadership of the Patriarch Arsenius Crnojevic III, left for exile in Hungary ... This was the beginning of the transfer of Serbia's religious, cultural and political centre of gravity Northwards, and finally to Belgrade.[24]

Wracked by internal conflict, and pressure from the great powers, Kosovo's remaining Orthodox Christians under Ottoman feudalism, managed to fuel the (re-)birth of Serbian nationalism. For Vickers, the 'continual evolution of the Serbian folk-epic was important in this period for the development of this national consciousness and instilled into it, apart from a spirit of revenge, against the Ottomans, an idealised memory of the Serbian past'.[25] Albeit voiced largely by illiterate folk-poets, this narrative gained momentum when, in 1804, a Serbian insurrection took hold.

The implications of the revolt were twofold. Noel Malcolm writes that although Ottoman forces did eventually re-conquer Serbia, a 'renewal of the revolt persuaded the Sultan to agree, in 1815, to give extensive powers of self-determination to a Serbian statelet under its *knez* or prince ... But its degrees of autonomy would grow, until, in 1878, when it was already the most powerful Christian state in the Balkans, its full independence would finally be recognized'.[26] While this fed into the story of Serbian revivalism, it also created the conditions in which the Ottoman authorities sought to arrest the decline into lawlessness in the Balkans, and reassert control over the unruly fiefdoms in South East Europe. Ottoman reforms were introduced in attempts to control provincial officials and bolster their control in the region. In the eyes of many locals, these reforms were viewed as repressive measures, drawing power back to the seat of the Porte in Turkey.

Kosovo remained a frontier region of sorts, given its location between expanding and contracting empires, particularly as the European Great Powers came to the fore. By the 1870s Bosnia-Herzegovina became the site of an uprising against the Ottomans, which eventually led to a plan of reform proposed by the Austro-Hungarians. The reform plan was designed to forestall intervention by the Russians, and at a local level in Kosovo led the Porte to encourage the 'Albanian population to settle scores with the local Slav-Orthodox element'.[27] The Ottoman Empire was in decline, and by 1877 what would become known as the League of Prizren asserted their authority, against the backdrop of the Russo-Ottoman war of the same year. Vicious fighting erupted, as waves of refugees and migrants fled. Although a truce had been signed by the Russian and Ottoman forces, by the end of January 1878 the Serbian army had captured the Monastery at Gracanica, near Pristina, where a 'liturgy was performed to honour' the Serbian victory and 'a commemoration was held for the heroes of 1389'.[28]

As the Ottoman Empire floundered, and following the defeat of the Porte in March 1878, Russian influence strengthened pan-Slavic revivalism. While Kosovo remained under the control of the Ottoman Turks, part of the San Stefano peace treaty afforded control over Albania to others. Some months prior to peace accord, the Turkish writer Abdyl Frashëri, encouraged by the Ottoman authorities, became the head of an Albanian autonomist movement. Following the declarations of San Stefano, Frashëri established a group known as the 'Central Committee for the Defence of the Rights of the Albanian Nation'. At its inaugural meeting – essentially building on the tradition of inter-clan meetings – in Prizren in June 1878, it was announced that a military-defensive formation, known as the 'League' would be formed, in order to 'stop any territory being occupied by foreign troops'.[29] A series of events followed which drove a wedge between the evolving idea of an autonomous Albanian region centring on Kosovo, and its re-integration into the declining Ottoman Empire. Sporadic revolts continued as harsh measures were deployed by the Porte to control Kosovo and the League, but, by the turn of the century a current of change had taken hold in the political centre of the Ottoman Empire as a semi-secret movement led by Mustafa Kemal Atatürk, which was to become known as the Young Turks, sought to overhaul the Ottoman system from within. 'When to try and win over the leaders of the Kosovo Albanians to their side. Almost the only strong common interest was the desire to resist the encroachments of foreign powers on the territory of the Empire: and by a lucky coincidence for the Young Turks, Kosovo was already in ferment over just that issue.'[30]

The short history of Kosovo offered here demonstrates how different national (Serbian and Albanian) movements emerged throughout the nineteenth and early part of the the twentieth centuries. Kosovo itself was seen as a site in a number of different competing narratives of ethnic and national identity. However, the migrations of peoples, the different religious, ethnic and local forms of social organisation meant that Kosovo itself had no central claim as an independent state. Instead Kosovo was at the centre of different emerging stories of national identity, framed by Great Power politics, as Empires formed and declined. In this way, Kosovo became storied, and as Chapter 3 argues, Kosovo from around the turn of the twentieth century became more politicised as the question of independence once again reared its head.

Chechnya/Ichkeria

The traditional home of the Chechen people is situated on the northern slopes of the mountain chain of the Caucasus. The Chechen republic is bordered to the south by Georgia, and flanked by other republics in the Russian Federation of Ingushetia and North Ossetia to the west, the province of Stavropol Krai to the North-West and, Dagestan to the east and north. Its size is around six thousand square miles and the population of just below one million people is largely Muslim. The complex historical backdrop to the continuing conflict is of particular importance because it illustrates how different forms of identity are produced. The first Russian incursion based on political expansionism in the North Caucasus occurred under the leadership of Ivan IV, in the mid-1550s. Thereafter the region was marked by continuous periods of struggle as different empires – the Persian, Ottoman, Russian and Soviet – sought to gain control of the North Caucasus.[31]

Interestingly, the conflicts were marked by brutal campaigns which throughout the eighteenth, nineteenth and twentieth centuries became infused with different forms of writing and narrative, from short stories or highlander poetry – to human rights reports and the written accounts of war correspondents.

Throughout the 1800s the North Caucasus – and Chechnya and Dagestan in particular – continued to be recognised as an area of confrontation between different political systems.[32] A succession of Russian military leaders sought to conquer and control the region. Each developed military and political strategies designed to undermine the resistance of the clans in Dagestan and Chechnya.[33] In so doing, the protracted period of conflict spawned a series of texts as a generation of Russian writers and poets wrote about the encounter in the North Caucasus. In these texts, a dominant Russian narrative of the 'Caucasian highlander' can be identified while the Caucasus is viewed by some literary specialists as Russia's 'Orient'.[34]

Indeed, the recent history of Chechnya indicates that insurrections led by Sufi Sheikhs and Imams also instituted a strict adherence and obedience to Sharia Law, in part indicating a well-defined and rigid structure that inscribed a cultural narrative of martyrdom, based around discipleship, kinship and family ties. In particular, *muridism* lent itself to a melding of religious identification and guerrilla war, in which discipleship, asceticism and mystical adherence to saints, helped to maintain morale, and generate social and political authority in many towns and villages in the North Caucasus.[35] This, coupled with the traditional customs, mores and forms of social and kin organisation in *teips*, that is, extended family, whose male members had responsibility for protecting the family, shaped the martial tradition within Chechen culture and played a considerable role in mobilisation in the first conflict.[36] For example, embedded within readings of mobilisation is the role of the *adat*, which helped to pass military knowledge from father to son, through generations.[37] Equally, a widely held belief in the role of blood relations, brotherhood, and the role of honour, or indeed, the notion that cowardice in war can bring shame on a family, led many to voice a willingness to choose death over dishonour, and fed into the establishment of units willing to die for the cause of Chechen separatism. If we take this point further, we can see that the turbulent historical relationship between the peoples of the Caucasus and Russia has long been woven into the literature, myths and legends.[38] In the case of Chechnya this draws attention to the role of alternative structures of social and cultural organisation such as the *teip*.[39] To put it bluntly: 'teips do not recognise the state and the state does not recognise the teips'.[40] These groupings – the clan, tribal and religious fabric of Chechen – Ingush relations – evoke certain customs and traditions such as the *aul* (home defence) or the blood feud which, in turn, influence the character of political violence.[41] These features of Chechen society, and many others besides, occur in contrast to modernity and the state. This is fair enough, provided we accept that, by refusing to particularise analysis, these features which operate as an aside to political discourses do influence global politics.

The age of empires: from Murids and Nationalists, to Communists and Separatists

Russian relations with groups in the North Caucasus have been marked by successive periods of war and conflict. The first extended period of conflict was shaped by the politics of empire, as Russia sought to extend its borders to the south, and challenge the regional influence of the Turks and the historical influence of the Persians. While the co-opting of non-Russian groups became an important part of the empire-building process, it was perhaps Russia's brutal military tactics, together with its failure to appreciate the mosaic of different ethnic groups in the mountain regions of the North Caucasus that ultimately led to an extended period of conflict. At the same time, though, an alliance of sorts emerged between the fiercely independent mountain-dwellers of the North Caucasus and Sufi adepts encouraging strict discipline, which together framed the resistance to Russian expansionism, giving rise to the first anti-Russian *ghazavat* (holy war, often designed to liberate lands from occupation).

The first *ghazavat* was led by Sheikh Ushurum, who has since become known as Sheikh Mansur. Sheikh Mansur plagued the Russian army from the 1780s, at first drawing support from fighters from the north-east of the Caucasus, and introducing the local population to Sufi Islam, proselytising groups in support of his *murid* movement. The *murids* were viewed as an almost 'monastic military Muslim order', who were obliged to obey the imam, or spiritual leader of the movement, and whose most 'sacred duty and object in life was to die in battle against the infidels'.[42] In other words, the ruthless insistence on obedience and the merger of highlander bravery with religious order created a potent force of highlander fighters capable of undertaking a drawn-out guerrilla campaign. Allen and Muratoff point out that the strength of the *murids* lay in their reading of 'war as the end in itself, as a vehicle for self-purification and self-sacrifice'.[43] The centre of anti-Russian radicalism began in Dagestan, but quickly drew on support from the Avars, Chechens and other Lesghi tribes, which coordinated their attacks to further undermine Russian control of the mountainous Caucasus.

Interestingly, reports indicate that Russian forces tried a range of tactics to subdue support for the uprisings, beyond simple military attacks. Thus, coercion and intimidation were supported by other means, such as attempts to divide and rule, in order to weaken the ability of the mountain villages or *auls* to resist the Russian advance. Moshe Gammer notes that, following Russian aggression and treachery, the call to arms, to holy war or *gazavat*, was 'answered by many Chechens and others, who flocked to [Mansur] at Aldy'.[44] Following a series of confrontations, and some intensive fighting in July and August 1785, Mansur retreated to the mountains, persuading the 'majority of the population of Lesser Kabarda to follow him'.[45] The regional and multi-ethnic character of the anti-Russian resistance, which included Kumyks, Chechens and other mountaineers, and also Dagestani fighters, was noted in reports by the Russian military at the time. And so Sheikh Mansur had managed to blend together an alliance of different ethnic groups by promoting Islam.

In the years after the uprising led by Sheikh Mansur, successive waves of resistance, culminating in a 30-year struggle between 1829 and 1859, led to the establishment of a number of unholy alliances. In this period the three imams, or leaders of the anti-Russian resistance, namely Ghazi Muhammad, Hamzat Bek and Shamil, were Dagestani.[46] On the one hand, the legacy of these imams helped to unify a fragmented society divided by 'tribal codes, clan and territorial affiliations and by the geographic terrain itself', overhauling and reforming the social and political order.[47] On the other hand, this signals the importance of Dagestani groups, shaping the spread of Islam in the North Caucasus, and, at least in part, uniting different ethnic groups under the banner of anti-Russian muridism. But the connections to the centres of Ottoman power, and indeed the broader field of power politics, were also intrinsic in developing an understanding of the alliances in this period. As Gammer notes, clear channels of communication operated between Chechen groups and the great powers throughout the 30-year uprising. Reports suggest that, towards the end of that three-decade insurrection, support was requested by Imam Shamil from both the British and the French.[48] Although channels of communication between Imam Shamil and Ottoman donors were also clearly established, Shamil – much like Sheikh Mansur – relied on a multi-national group of local supporters, shifting his struggle from Dagestan into Chechnya before eventually surrendering to the overwhelming power of Russian forces. While Shamil remains the keystone in the Chechen anti-Russian narrative, his surrender in 1859 did not end the guerrilla war, with one of his *naibs* (lieutenants), Baysungur from Benoy, continuing to fight for a further two years.[49]

In the latter part of the nineteenth century, following the end of the 30-year struggle, successive attempts were made to incorporate North Caucasian groups into the Russian army. For instance, an irregular cavalry unit, named *terskii konnyi polk* (Terek [Irregular] Cavalry Regiment) was formed in 1860, made up of enlisted Chechens, while militias from the indigenous population were organised in an attempt to enrol 'the most restless elements of Chechnya, Ichkeria, and Aukh and remove them, with their horses and weapons, as far as possible from the confines of the country'.[50] However, attempts to raise and employ local militias in this period largely failed, with Chechen fighters often deserting or joining rebel groups still fighting the Russian forces.[51] None the less, the ever-changing allegiances in this period were themselves consumed in the tides of historical change, as the First World War in Europe led to the end of the Russian and Ottoman Empires.

'For Soviet power – for Shariat'

In the period of the Russian Civil War, from late 1917 through to mid-1920, events in the North Caucasus were marked by 'ever-changing alliances on the battlefield'.[52] In the admixture, mountain dwellers, Red Partisans, Cossacks, Turks, Georgian Mensheviks and murids all played a role, as did the varying levels of foreign intervention in the region. In particular, the confrontation between White Russian forces centring on Denikin, and Red Partisan fighters also shaped the events on the battlefields in the Caucasus, leading to temporary alliances and changing coalitions.

However, in late 1917 the Bolsheviks adopted another strategy off the battlefield, designed to undermine the threat posed by a unified anti-communist stance across differing ethnic communities by setting up the People's Commissariat of Nationalities (the *Narkomnats*). Located within the

Commissariat of Nationalities, the department named *Muskom*, or Muslim Committee, engaged in enticing the Muslim population into the Soviet system by granting them autonomy. This approach led to the promotion of Muslim revolutionary leaders, including Mulla-Nur Vahitov and Mir Said Sultan-Galiev, whose support was garnered to bolster the Bolshevik cause. These 'Muslim Communists' became members of the Muslim Socialist Committee, seeking to amend and transform the Bolshevik movement from within, so as to address the dire socio-economic conditions of Muslims in the Soviet Union. Their work led to a series of documents and the establishment of a Central Bureau of Muslim Communists, which included a specifically Muslim unit of the Russian Communist Party.[53] The Bolshevik cause thus gained some support from a number of Muslim clerics in the North Caucasus, who became known as the 'Red Shariatists' and whose slogan was 'For Soviet Power – for Shariat'.

In 1917 Russia had a significant Muslim population, which was divided in its response to the Bolshevik revolution. While groups including the *qadimists* rejected the legitimacy of Bolshevik power, others such as the Vaisities in the Volga–Urals region, who preached a form of ultra-traditionalism, formed a tactical alliance with the Bolsheviks in order to counter the Islamist nationalist movements of the Soviet south. Reformists within the Islamic community, known as the jadids, were similarly divided in their attitudes towards the Bolsheviks. While many simply confined themselves to life under Bolshevik rule, a number of the reformists who opposed the Bolsheviks were organised by Muslim leaders such as Mufti Galimzian Barudi into Islamic regiments which joined the White Army to fight against the spread of Communism. Interestingly, as Alexandre Bennigsen notes,

> between 1917 and 1920 in the North Caucasus, the leadership of the revolutionary movement belonged to Muslim radicals who had joined the Bolshevik Party rather than Russian Communists. These native Bolsheviks belonged to the upper levels of Muslim society and their ancestors fought the Russians under Shamil (Makhach Dakhadaev was married to a granddaughter of Shamil). They were certainly dedicated communists and loyal to the Bolshevik leadership but remained nationalist and did not underestimate the vital role of Islam in the North Caucasus.[54]

Another legacy of this period was the idea of a North Caucasus Republic, known as *Gorskaya Respublika* (Mountain Republic), partly financed by the Grozny millionaire Tapa Chermoyev. Capitalizing on the Tsar's resignation, in mid-May 1917 the mountain dwellers held a congress aimed at unifying their peoples under a self-governing body. Headed by Russian-educated elites, the body included representatives from the Kabardians, Balkars, Chechens, Dagestanis and Ossetians and most of them conceived of the new alliance in secular–democratic terms. However, the Sufi orders pressed for the Shari'a as the governing principle as it was they who could mobilise large numbers of men.[55] Yet General Denikin refused to recognize any independent states in the region and used force to bring the Mountain Republic to an end. The Kumyk politician Haidar Bammate who represented the short-lived Gorskaya Respublika at the Paris Peace Conference, drew attention to the multi-ethnic nature of the North Caucasus Republic.[56]

This reality led a number of prominent Chechen leaders to favour the Bolsheviks, particularly as they had encouraged their self-determination and freedom of religious expression, in a peculiar precursor to Yeltsin's fateful proclamation at the century's end. Despite a firm alliance between the Bolsheviks and some Chechen and Dagestani religious leaders, in response to the failure of the Mountain Republic in September 1919 the elderly Naqshbandi Sheikh Uzen Haji al-Salty pronounced an Emirate of the North Caucasus, centred upon the Shari'a. Based in Vedeno, Uzen Haji declared jihad against Denikin's forces, uniting both secular and religious figures in this endeavour. Furnishing himself with the title Imam, his declaration mirrored the long-standing anti-Russian resistance in the region, particularly given his selection of Vedeno as the emirate's capital and its administrative partition into seven *na'ib-doms*.[57] The uprising was neither nationalist nor political, but instead drew support as a religious movement that sought to expel infidels and establish a theocratic imamate, under the suzerainty of the Ottoman caliphate, mirroring the earlier attempts by Shamil to organise the different groups in the region under the banner of Islam.

Indeed, the movement garnered support from the long-standing network of Circassians and Chechens based in Turkey. This led Imam Shamil's great grandson Said-Bek to travel from Turkey to Chechnya in support of the guerrilla war, highlighting links between external groups in Turkey and the anti-Russian resistance that resurfaced in the post-Soviet era. However, the history of the emirate was short-lived, as Uzen Haji died in 1920. Although resistance to the Bolsheviks continued, particularly through the actions of the Avar Najmuddin of Hötso and Sayyid Amin of Ansalta, by the mid-1920s they had largely quelled opposition in the Caucasus.[58]

Equally, throughout the period of early Soviet rule we can identify a number of events that have shaped episodes of Russo-Chechen violence. In the early 1920s the Bolshevik Party had devised a strategy of divide and rule, drawing on the different ethnic groups and religious systems in the North Caucasus, turning the Ingush against the Chechens, and exploiting cleavages between the different forms of Sufism (Naqshbandiyya and Qadiriyya) with the Qadiriyya Ali Mitaev becoming a member of the Chechen Revolutionary Committee known as Revkom (*Revolyutsionnyi komitet*) – another point mirrored in the post-Soviet period as the Qadiriya Mufti Akhmed Kadyrov chose to align himself with Putin's Russian administration. By the late 1930s many of these pro-Bolshevik leaders (including Najmuddin Samurskii, an outspoken nationalist who became First Secretary of the Communist Party in Dagestan) had been executed in the Stalinist purges.

Then, in 1941, the ideological battle between Soviet Russia and Nazi Germany placed the North Caucasus in the middle of a wider ideological confrontation. As the war turned in favour of Russia a policy of targeting specific ethnic groups which, it was claimed, had sympathised with the Nazi forces, was put into action. The Chechens, along with other ethnic groups, were forcibly deported to other parts of Soviet Russia.[59] While many of the Chechens were repatriated after Stalin's death, the event fed into the desire for independence from Communist Russia, a point that would resurface in the latter part of the Cold War as totalitarian rule and political ideologies crumbled in 1980s (see Chapter 3). In short, stories flag-up encounter, similarity and difference, helping to frame narratives of identity which connect deep histories with more contemporary concerns, fears and anxieties, or heroic deeds and celebrations of pride. Albeit implicitly then, these stories help to shape action.

Conclusion

Chapter 1 staked out a theoretical framework which drew upon interpretive or hermeneutic approaches to global politics. In order to support this argument, this chapter has demonstrated that a more nuanced account of political violence is essential if IR is to shed light on contemporary conflict, and the phenomenon of war. Indeed drawing on the role of myths, and of the narratives associated with particular conflicts, it has demonstrated how the interpretive framework of Chapter 1 can be employed to enrich studies of war. This does much to reinforce the notion that accounts of new wars are insightful but lack a thoroughgoing historical grounding and perhaps require more empirical research to support the claims made in this literature.

Notes

1   H. Suganami, 'Agents, Structures, Narratives', *European Journal of International Relations*, Vol. 5, No. 3 (1999), p. 380.
2   C. Hedges, *War Is A Force That Gives Us Meaning* (Oxford: Public Affairs, 2002), p. 21.
3   *Ibid.*, p. 23.
4   G. Schöpflin, 'The Functions of Myths and a Taxonomy of Myths', in G. Hosking

and G. Schöpflin (eds.), *Myths and Nationhood* (London: Hurst & Co, 1997), p. 19.

5   G. Schöpflin, 'The Nature of Myth: Some Theoretical Aspects', in S. Schwandner-Sievers and B.J. Fischer (eds.), *Albanian Identities: Myth and History* (Bloomington, IN: Indiana University Press, 2002), p. 29.

6   *Ibid.*, pp. 29–30.

7   Schöpflin, 'The Function of Myths', pp. 19–20.

8   *Ibid.*, pp. 19–28.

9   *Ibid.*, p. 20.

10 See V. Pshvela, 'Host and Guest', in M. Kvesselava (ed.), *Georgian Poetry* (Tbilisi: Akolasia, 2004), pp. 80–90.

11 G-R. Sabri-Tabrizi, 'Chechnya and the Impact of the Chechen Conflict on Russia, the CIS and Iran', in A. Mohammadi and A. Ehteshami (eds.), *Iran and Eurasia* (Reading: Garnet, 2000), p. 170.

12 R. Barthes, *Mythologies* (Paris: Seuil, 1957).

13 A. Pennington and P. Levi, trans, *Marko The Prince: Serbo-Croat Heroic Songs* (London: Duckworth Press, 1984), p. xiv.

14 N. Malcolm, *Kosovo: A Short History* (Basingstoke: Macmillan, 1998), pp. xxxiv–xxxv.

15 G. Duijzings, *Religion and the Politics of Identity in Kosovo* (New York: Columbia University Press, 2000).

16 Malcolm, *Kosovo*.

17 Duijzings, *Religion and the Politics of Identity*, p. 6.

18 *Ibid.*, pp. 6–7.

19 The Battle of Kosovo is often referred as a metaphor for the demise of Serbia. It is referenced in poetry, myth or literature as the 'Field of the Black Crows', producing a visceral image of birds flocking to the scene of the battle to pick at the bodies of the dead and dying combatants. The metaphor is thus represented in a way which has emotional meaning. The evocation of the Field of the Black Crows may be said to be communicative, referring to the loss, pain, suffering and indignity of the Serbian people. It also conjures up emotive meaning through affective imagery; it is a visual depiction of the loss of Serbian honour providing a powerful symbolic representation which was to shape social and political identity claims.

20 Pennington and Levi, *Marko the Prince*, pp. viii–ix.

21 Malcolm, *Kosovo*, p. 58.

22 *Ibid.*

23 Malcolm, *Kosovo*.

24 M. Vickers, *Between Serb and Albanian: A History of Kosovo* (London: Hurst & Co., 1998), p. 27.

25 *Ibid.*, pp. 29–30.

26 Malcolm, *Kosovo*, p. 180.

27 Vickers, *Between Serb and Albanian*, p. 42.

28 *Ibid.*, p. 43.

29 Malcolm, *Kosovo*, p. 221.

30 *Ibid.*, p. 237.

31 See, for instance, W.E.D. Allen and P. Muratoff, *Caucasian Battlefields: A History*

of the Wars on the Turco-Caucasian Border 1828-1921 (Cambridge: Cambridge University Press, 1953).

32 A. Zelkina, *In Quest for God and Freedom: Sufi Responses to the Russian Advance in the North Caucasus* (London: Hurst & Co, 2000); M. Gammer, *Muslim Resistance to the Tsar: Shamil and the Conquest of Chechnia and Daghestan* (London: Frank Cass, 2005).

33 M. Gammer, *The Lone Wolf and the Bear: Three Centuries of Chechen Defiance of Russian Rule* (London: Hurst & Co, 2006).

34 S. Layton, *Russian Literature and Empire: Conquest of the Caucasus from Pushkin to Tolstoy* (Cambridge: Cambridge University Press, 1994).

35 For instance, see M. Bennigsen Broxup, 'The Last Ghazawat: The 1920–1921 Uprising', in *The North Caucasus Barrier: The Russian Advance Towards the Muslim World* (London: Hurst & Co, 1992), pp. 112–145.

36 This point was raised in interviews with Chechen participants and observers from the first war, and indeed, foreign correspondents who covered the conflict. In an interview with Sebastian Smith, author of *Allah's Mountains*, in Tbilisi in September 2004 he noted that 'scores of people, including men, women and children came onto the streets to build barricades' at the outset of the conflict.

37 *Adat* refers to the idea of customary law. It can be used in either the pan-Caucasian context or in a Chechen version, taking into account national peculiarities. In effect then, the code that is the *adat* refers to customs and rules which govern different spheres of life, such as loyalty to the *teip*, but also to *nokchalla* (the quality of being Chechen), thereby having influence on individual and collective modes of behaviour.

38 Of course numerous other examples exist than those discussed here. For example, L. Tolstoy, *The Cossacks* (New York: Everyman's Library, 1994); J. Steinbeck with photographs by R. Capa, *A Russian Journal* (Harmondsworth: Penguin, 1999); L. Tolstoy, *War and Peace* (London: Penguin Classics, 2006).

39 M. Vachagayev, 'Sovremennoye Chechenskoye Obshchestvo', *Tsentral'naya Azia I Kavkaz*, No. 2 (2003), p. 16.

40 Y. Chesnov, 'Byt Chechentsem: Lichnost i etnicheskiye identifikatsii naroda', in D. Furman (ed.), *Chechnya i Rossiya: obshchestva i gosudarstva* (Moscow: Andrei Sakharov Foundation, 1999), pp. 63–101.

41 The meaning, and indeed the impact of the *teip* system, is however, contested. See the ethnographic accounts of the two wars: A. Lieven, *Chechnya: Tombstone of Russian Power* (New Haven, CT: Yale University Press, 1998); E. Souliemanov, *An Endless War: The Russian–Chechen Conflict in Perspective* (Oxford: Peter Lang, 2007), and E. Sokirianskaya, 'Families and Clans in Ingushetia and Chechnya: A Fieldwork Report', *Central Asian Survey*, Vol. 24, No. 4 (2005), pp. 453–467. It is clear though that both the *teip* system, and indeed, *auls* played a role in shaping the nature and form of violence in the region in the two conflicts of the 1990s.

42 Allen and Muratoff, *Caucasian Battlefields*, p. 48.

43 *Ibid.*, p. 48.

44 Gammer, *The Lone Wolf and the Bear*, p. 23.

45 *Ibid.*, p. 23.

46 Ibid., pp. 31–103.

47   Zelkina, *In Quest for God and Freedom*, p. 235.

48   M. Gammer, *Muslim Resistance to the Tsar: Shamil and the Conquest of Chechnia and Daghestan* (London: Hurst & Co, 2005), p. 285.

49   M. Gammer, 'Nationalism and History: Rewriting the Chechen National Past', in B. Coppieters and M. Huysseune (eds.), *Secession, History and the Social Sciences* (Brussels: VUB Brussels University Press, 2002), p. 126.

50   This point was noted in a report by Count Mikhail Loris-Melikov, Commander-in-Chief of the Russian forces in the Terek province in the 1870s, cited in Gammer *The Lone Wolf and the Bear*, p. 73.

51   Gammer, *The Lone Wolf and the Bear*, p. 71.

52   Bennigsen-Broxup, 'The Last Ghazawat', pp. 112–145.

53   G. Yemelianova, *Russia and Islam: A Historical Survey* (London: Routledge, 2002), pp. 102–103.

54   A. Bennigsen, 'Muslim Guerrilla Warfare in the Caucasus (1918–1928)', *Central Asian Survey*, Vol. 2, No. 1 (1983), p. 48.

55   Gammer, *The Lone Wolf and the Bear*, pp. 120–122.

56   Bammate's speech was republished in English in the early 1990s: see H. Bammate, 'The Caucasus and the Russian Revolution (from a Political Viewpoint)', *Central Asian Survey*, Vol. 10, No. 4 (1991), pp. 1–29.

57   Gammer, *The Lone Wolf and the Bear*, pp. 130–131.

58   Bennigsen, 'Muslim Guerilla Warfare', pp. 45–56.

59   R. Conquest, *The Nation Killers* (London: Macmillan, 1970); B.G. Williams, 'Commemorating "The Deportation" in Post-Soviet Chechnya: The Role of Memorialization and Collective Memory in the 1994–1996 and 1999–2000 Russo-Chechen Wars', *History & Memory*, Vol. 12, No. 1 (2000), pp. 101–134.

3

Regional politics, trans-local identity and history

This chapter introduces some background themes which influence the networks, groups and affiliations, and latterly distinctive armed resistance movements, in the Balkans and the Caucasus in the mid-1990s. In both cases the armed resistance movements emerged against the backdrop of the disintegration of the USSR and Socialist Yugoslavia, but the provenance of each movement needs to be located in a broader frame of late nineteenth- and twentieth-century history. The armed resistance movements became involved in low-level conflicts in Kosovo and Chechnya, and more generally in the neighbouring regions and environs. A number of revolts and insurrections were repeated in the newly independent states in the Balkans and Caucasus, eventually leading to a full-scale nationalist-separatist Russo-Chechen War (1994–1996) and a conflict between Serbia and Bosnian militias (1992–1995).

The chapter begins by tracing some of the salient features of the recent history of Kosovo and Chechnya, highlighting how particular events in the twentieth century shaped the different resistance movements. Chapter 2 drew attention to the deep history which has shaped more recent development in the post-Communist period in the North Caucasus. More specifically, in the first Russo-Chechen war of the 1990s the Chechen resistance formed around a separatist ideal, shaped by the memory of the Stalinist deportations in 1944. It is essential, however, to draw attention to a longer historical period in the Balkans, given that the era of Great Power politics played a significant role in shaping post-Communist nationalist movements and thus influenced the violence that erupted as Yugoslavia fragmented. In the Cold War, the Kosovar Albanian separatist movement was largely framed by differences between the two Communist regimes of Yugoslavia and Albania, and prior to this Great Power politics, the crumbling of the Ottoman Empire in the early part of the twentieth century, and the emergence of Serbian and Albanian nationalism in the latter part of the nineteenth century. While these parallels go some way to explain how the violent resistance emerged in the early 1990s, this chapter also demonstrates how regional politics framed some aspects of each movement, and sheds light on the differences between the two movements. As already argued, this is important insofar as narratives are concerned, precisely because it is the interconnection between events and the 'operation of configuration' which gives these events meaning. In both Kosovo and Chechnya, and in both respective armed resistance movements, it is the characters and interconnections, partly made possible by globalisation and the end of the Cold War, alongside the regional dynamics, which read through the lens of 'trans-local identity' give insight into the diverse groups which formed the KLA and the units of Chechen Republic of Ichkeria.

The Balkans: from Great Powers to Communism

The Balkans continued to be a site of insurrection, with a series of revolts and various uprisings in Kosovo, albeit short-lived and localised, also being reflected in broader debates about the status of the region at the epicentre of Great Power politics. Noel Malcolm notes that the 'general conditions in Kosovo in the 1880s and 1890s were very poor' with changes imposed by the Ottomans, creating a new *vilayet* of Kosovo.[1] The general deterioration in religious relations was heightened by mass expulsions in 'Muslim lands taken over by Serbia, Bulgaria and Montenegro in 1877–8'.[2] These mass migrations from parts of Serbia were coupled with the movement of refugees into and the emigration of Serbs out of Kosovo. At the international level, the influence of the Ottoman Turks continued to decline, while new Slav nationalist movements sprung up in the South Balkans, producing a general sense of unease in the region. In short, the 'pressure exerted by the Great Powers and Ottoman state tended to increase suspicions and hostilities of Albanians towards their Christian neighbours'.[3]

By 1908, within the Ottoman Empire, the Young Turks began the process of constitutional reform. For a short time at least this had the effect of pacifying the sporadic revolts which had blighted Kosovo. However, deep divisions did emerge between the Albanians and Ottomans as 'the Albanians continued to advocate more decentralization of the Empire and autonomy for their national regions, while the Young Turks adopted a series of measures designed to reinforce central power'.[4] Meanwhile the influence of Russia and Austria-Hungary forced Serbia to seek alliances to ensure her newly found status remained intact. At the same time, disillusionment with the reforms of the Young Turks drove them into a 'series of wars which united against them all the national and separatist forces it contained'.[5] By the summer of 1909 Muslim clans in Kosovo were in open rebellion against the Young Turks, who appointed Djavid Pasha as military commandant in the Mitrovica region in order to suppress the revolt. The turmoil and subsequent reign of terror throughout 1910 prompted the Russian authorities to warn the Ottoman Turks against the extension of hostilities towards Macedonians. Tens of thousands of Serbs fled Kosovo, according to reports, throughout 1911, as Ottoman rule crumbled. In September Italy declared war on the Porte, and by the summer of 1912, Serbia was actively involved in establishing and supporting Albanian armed revolts, in order to weaken Ottoman influence on the region. For Vickers the Young Turks had overlooked the 'growing national sentiments of the Albanians', handling their grievances insensitively.[6] The creation of a form of Albanian nationalism borne out of the League of Prizren, coupled with the decline in Ottoman influence, led to the first Balkan War.

By 1911 a Balkan League comprised of Bulgaria, Greece, Serbia and Montenegro had formed, which – with encouragement from Russia – sought to divide the European Ottoman territory between themselves. By mid-1912, to the surprise of the newly formed Balkan League, groups of Albanian nationalists in Ottoman territories made a claim for national consideration by the Great Powers, pre-empting the onslaught to 'liberate' the land of Kosovo by the Balkan alliance. This ultimately led to the outbreak of the first Balkan War in October 1912, as Montenegro attacked Albanian territory. Vickers notes, the outbreak of war led thousands of Serbian volunteers to join the army

> yearning to avenge the Battle of Kosovo. The declaration of war had opened up the exalting prospect of participating in national rebirth – an ideal bequeathed to them by their forefathers. The realization that Kosovo might be liberated after more than five centuries fired their imaginations and emotions, and the Serbian army was unstoppable ... With a profound sense of national elation Serbian troops finally entered Pristina on the 22nd of October.[7]

Albanian forces, who had by then sided with the Ottoman Turks, continued to resist in and around Kosovo (particularly the key leaders Isa Botetini and Bajram Curri), however they were ultimately defeated as an organised political force as the Ottoman Empire entered its final days. The position and status of Kosovo remained unresolved until the Conference of Ambassadors convened in December 1912, in order to debate the status and organisation of an independent state of Albania. The negotiations were fraught with difficulties as concessions and counterweights were variously sought by Russia,

Austro-Hungary, and Serbia in order to halt the fighting as the Ottoman Empire fell apart. An explicit desire also existed which sought to prevent the escalation of the first Balkan War into a broader conflict between the Great Powers. By 1913, the Balkan allies had signed a peace agreement with the Sublime Porte, essentially defeating the Ottoman Empire, leading to the creation of an Albanian state, but also leaving a considerable portion of the Albanian peoples outside the borders of the state. In sum, for 'the Albanians the actions of the Young Turks had driven and speeded up their national movement'.[8] And yet, the new Albanian state – without swaths of Kosovo – remained nascent, located as it was in precarious geopolitical position between the Balkan allies, protected by 'the vague benevolence of a distant assembly of patriarchs'.[9]

The political turmoil once again led to the mass migrations of peoples from Kosovo, with some reports estimating that as many as 120,000 Albanians left Kosovo between 1913 and 1915.[10] Two further events occurred in the period after the end of the First World War (1914–1918) which engulfed Europe, and at the end of the Second World War (1939–1945). Before returning to this period it is worth summarising some key themes, first, Serbian and Albanian national movements emerged throughout the nineteenth century, which tied a sense of belonging to oral traditions, ballads and myths surrounding Kosovo; second, Serbian and Albanian national movements were formed in the midst of the rise and fall of other empires; and finally, that the status of Kosovo – including a specific narrative of Kosovar Albanian identity – remained either unresolved or unformed.

These points were neither resolved, nor fundamentally altered by two further contextual historical points; firstly, the Albanian population of the region resisted incorporation into Yugoslavia as it was inaugurated at the end of the First World War in 1918, and secondly, many years later the Albanian population resisted incorporation in the federal, and soon to be Communist state of Yugoslavia in 1944.

Kosova and Communism: between Tito and Hoxa

The Balkan Federation – in essence an arm of the Communist International – aided the regional nationalist policies of groups opposed to Yugoslavia. The Balkan Federation supported the actions of the Kosova Committee (*Komeiteti e Kosovës*) or KK in its attempts to instigate mass armed resistance to Serbian rule. Stephen Schwartz writes that the Kosova Committee

> anticipated the latter KLA-UÇK in lacking an elaborated platform, aside from Albanian nationalism, or even the demands of an economic reform programme.

While the KK was led by the outstanding Kosvar patriots of the time, such as the long active anti-Serbian combatant Bajram Curri (1862–1925), it had no social-revolutionary content, and indeed was viewed by most observers as defending the property rights of traditional Muslim landlords.[11]

For the most part Kosova was occupied with resistance having been subdued by German forces in April 1941. Most of the region was controlled by Italian forces under the command of Mussolini, and the aegis of the Axis Powers. The town of Mitrovica remained under German control as an autonomous region of Serbia, given its important coal reserves and the existent mining facilities around the town.

The two forms of Communism adopted by the respective parties in Albania and Yugoslavia in the period after the end of Second World War did much to shape a sense of autonomy and identity within Kosovo itself. In Yugoslavia the style of Communism adopted by the Party leader Josef Tito sought to sanction against the nationalist sentiments, given the multiplicity of ethnic groups that made up the Yugoslav state. Thus Tito rallied against Croat, Serb and Albanian nostalgia – and yearning for more pronounced ethnic rights – in an attempt to unify the respective constituent parts of Yugoslavia and maintain a multiethnic federal system of rule. While the region remained within the federation of units which made up Yugoslavia, the close ties to their kinfolk and brethren across the border in Hoxa's Albania were stifled by party dogmatism. In contrast to the Yugoslav attempts to adopt and instil a form of ethnic consciousness and federalism, the Albanian Party of Labour embraced a cult of personality bolstered by a form of nationalist Communism. But these different cleavages – and the labels of Titoist and Enverist attached to them – had little bearing on the formation of the UCK-Kosovo Liberation Army. The terms were, as one academic noted, 'as dead as the men with which they originated'.[12]

Kosovo: towards the abyss: 1974–1987

Albeit suppressed by Communism, Kosovo's position between Serbia and Albania, the long-standing claims to parts of the region, and the limited autonomy first granted and later rescinded, produced competing claims for an independent Kosova. To some extent, the forging of the state-let of Kosova resulted from the geopolitical location of Kosovo on the border between Yugoslavia and Albania, alongside its administration within Yugoslavia between the early 1970s and late 1990s. The latter period from the mid-1980s will be discussed in Chapter 4, but first, it is important to consider two political events which helped to produce a Kosovar narrative of identity. The first event in 1974 occurred when Yugoslavia was still under the control of

Marshall Tito, as part of a broader package of political reforms. In an attempt to reform the Yugoslav politics and yet retain a multi-ethnic federal system, following an upsurge in internal discontent with the system in the late 1960s, a new constitution was rolled out on 21 February 1974. This narrowed the powers of the Federation, while simultaneously extending the powers of the republics and autonomous provinces.

In effect, this changed the status of Kosovo – one of the two autonomous provinces – granting it a series of rights and privileges as a constitutive element of the Federation of Socialist Republics of Yugoslavia. The constitutional changes occurred against the backdrop of a wave of student demonstrations in 1968 across Europe, including some behind the Iron Curtain. Within the demonstrations calls were heard for more minority rights, and for the overthrow of what was perceived by a small minority of students as the colonial control of Kosova. The authorities responded by establishing a university in Prishtina/Pristina, and improving the situation of the Kosovar Albanians. Other moves included the 'use of Albanian Professors and Albanian textbooks to teach Albanian language and literature, rapid Albinization of administration and security and increased public investment'.[13] The political changes resulted in the aforementioned constitutional reform, granting the administrative region an assembly, a judiciary and membership of the federal Parliament, in which it had the right of veto.

In effect this process led to the rapid growth in aspirations, including those linked to furthering independence. However muted, the growth of the University in Pristina and the awareness of an Albanian heritage partly influenced by Tirana 'fed nationalist aspirations'.[14]

In essence this led to the creation of a small, clandestine Kosovar movement in the late 1970s. For instance, in 1978, celebrations occurred to mark the founding of the League of Prizren, in part gesturing towards the seminal event in the narrative of Albanian nationalism. Then in 1981, Kosovo witnessed widespread student riots following Tito's death. A state of emergency was declared and the protests were quickly crushed, with military and police units arresting hundreds of people. For some writers, the 'period of the late 1960s and 1970s, which were often considered the apogee of the Tito period and to which both Albanians and Serbs were to look back nostalgically, were over. The consequence was a growing polarization between the Albanian and Serbian communities in Kosovo during the 1980s'.[15] The unravelling of this system of centralised rule, coupled with the informed sense of sacrifice, and the emerging socio-cultural forces such as globalisation, gave Kosovar resistance a particular form.

In sum, inter-generational change in the Kosovar Albanian movement, alongside the end of Communism combined with growing nationalist sentiments in Albania and Serbia influenced the creation of an armed movement, which sought to wrest control of Kosova from Serbia throughout the 1990s. Elsewhere, in the Caucasus a different chain of events led to the creation of an armed resistance movement, which would become involved in a war with the Russian authorities in 1999.

Chechnya 1989–1994: towards the abyss

The idea of a unified North Caucasus governing entity was rekindled as the Soviet Union began to unravel. Its genesis was rooted in the emergent nationalist sentiment fomenting throughout the Soviet Union in the late 1980s.[16] A reawakening of ethnic identity drew attention to not only the Soviets' oppression of the small nations but, more widely, also that of the Tsars, pushing dissent steadily throughout the dozens of ethnic groups in the North Caucasus.

In August 1989 the Abkhaz authorities invited an array of personalities from across the North Caucasus to a meeting at which the Confederation of Mountain Peoples of the North Caucasus (KGNK) was formally established. The Kabardin dissident intellectual Musa Shanib was elected as head. The new Confederation's principal aim was the re-establishment of a secular North Caucasian republic, united by a common highlander culture and shared history of Russian repression.[17] Known as the KGNK, the Confederation rejected the stance of the incumbent authorities, with the exception of Chechnya, whose new revolutionary leadership was striving to fulfil the 'nationalistic wishes and aspirations of the majority of the populace'.[18] The aim of the KGNK was political change, informed by popular nationalistic sentiments. The fragmentation of the Soviet Union, and the attempt to re-federalise former Soviet republics, provided the backdrop for the actions of the KGNK. Shanib, a native of the capital of Kabardino-Balkaria Nal'chik, had spent much of his early years establishing a career as a district attorney on the periphery of the Soviet bureaucratic elite. However he forfeited his career as a law-enforcement official, and instead took up a position as a junior lecturer, working towards a dissertation on the role of law and socialist self-governance. In the late 1960s, due to his stance towards the Soviet authorities, Shanib had become known locally as a dissident. Many years later, as the Soviet Union collapsed, Shanib's star rose, as he attempted to mobilise and harness militant nationalism to a common end. The movement was initially unremarkable, primarily because its leading exponents were preoccupied dislodging or jockeying with the extant Soviet authorities and rival groupings in their respective republics. However, in 1992, at the instigation of the movement's leading Chechen figures Zelimkhan Yandarbiyev and its notorious Vice President, Yusup Soslambekov, it was galvanised into armed resistance to the Georgians' perceived aggression against the Abkhaz.

The Parliament of the KGNK, along with the International Circassian Association and the Congress of the Kabardin People, began to mobilise groups in support of the Abkhaz. In the weeks that followed, at least two thousand 'Abaza, Adigean, Cherkess, Kabardian and Chechen volunteers joined forces with Abkhaz army units'.[19] The KGNK provided the rubric under which an array of local ethnic groups believed they could unite, drawing on a pool of young disaffected volunteers searching for a role within the post-Soviet North Caucasus.[20]

Elsewhere, a group of Communist party members watched the events in Moscow, supporting neither Gorbachov nor his challengers. Instead, this group of former Communist party officials seized the opportunity to become powerbrokers within Chechnya proper. Largely drawing on the Communist party *nomenklatura* and the Russian-speaking population, their tribal affiliations and support networks in the Northern plains of Chechnya, a group of pro-Moscow Chechens garnered support and challenged the growing nationalist drive of the early 1990s. This group was composed of an admixture of Chechens, including Doku Zavgayev and Umar Avtorkhanov from the Northern plains, as well as former Dudayev loyalists such as Bislan Gantemirov and Ruslan Labazanov.

The Abkhaz battalion and beyond

The paramilitary group formed by the KGNK became known as the 'volunteer peace-keeping battalion of the Mountain Confederation'. The battalion was composed of Cherkess, Kabardins, Adygheans and the largest unit of around five hundred Chechen volunteers.[21] In a further ironic twist, these units, particularly those under the then unknown Chechen commanders Ruslan Gelayev and Shamil Basayev, were overtly trained and funded by elements of Russian military intelligence, Glavnoye Razvedyvatel'noye Upravleniye (GRU), who sought to harness their fervour by displacing them from the North Caucasus and utilising them as proxies in a war against the newly independent Georgia. Ruslan Gelayev's early involvement in leading the volunteer units on behalf of the Abkhaz against the Georgians serves to underline the constantly shifting alliances within the region.[22] The Confederation also received significant support from the Circassian Diaspora and the Turkish Ministry of Defence.[23]

The Confederation's unifying ideology gradually divided between the largely ethno-nationalist aims of the Circassian Abkhaz, Cherkess, Adygh and Kabardin elements versus the more overtly religious Chechens who expounded an increasingly violent anti-Russian ideology. Those Sovietised Confederation leaders such as Shanib struggled to reconcile these distinctions while the mostly pagan Abkhaz quickly tired of the Chechen presence. It was at this juncture that the common cause of the Confederation's constituent ethnic groups splintered under Chechen dominance and religiosity.

The Abkhaz experience formed the basis of the local and international networks that Basayev would utilise over the coming decade to take the fight to Russia and beyond during both the first and second Russo-Chechen Wars. As an illustration, the leader of a pro-Chechen group based in Turkey, Muhammed Tockan, had participated in the Abkhaz War, where he became affiliated with Basayev. Tockan had then returned to Turkey, but took an active role clandestinely supporting the Chechen separatist movement from afar. Then, in 1996, he led a group of pro-Chechen hostage-takers in an attack on a Russian ferry near the Turkish port town of Trabzon to highlight the Chechens' plight.

By late 1993 the resolution of Yeltsin's battle with the parliament stabilised the majority of the North Caucasus republics, and they settled into regimes largely dominated by elites from the indigenous ethnic groups. The idea of a unified Mountainous Republic had again had its moment in history. Yeltsin now turned his attention to the rapidly deteriorating situation in Chechnya under the leadership of Soviet Air Force General Jokhar Dudayev. Ironically, Chechen society had initially backed Yeltin's opposition to the Communist authorities, with the young Shamil Basayev himself manning the barricades in Moscow in support.

Nationalists vs. Islamists

The Soviet collapse was accompanied by intense Islamic revivalism across the North Caucasus, where the secretive Sufi Brotherhoods had survived and thrived, despite the best efforts of the Soviet authorities to quell their influence.[24] A new key actor to emerge in the region was the All-Union Islamic Renaissance Party (IRP). Founded in Astrakhan in 1990, the party's original members included the Dagestani Bagautdin Kebedov, whose brother has taught at Al-Azhar University in Cairo, the Chechen doctor Islam Khalimov and the Chechen ideologist Movladi Udugov and his brother Isa Umarov. These individuals formed the original core of the indigenous Salafi network in the region. While their message was yet to be heard amidst the mass mobilisation of the nationalist-separatist Chechen movement in the first half of the 1990s their power has increased exponentially and became the dominant influence over the ideology of the Chechen-led North Caucasus resistance in 2008.

Much of Chechnya's senior leadership during the first war were born in exile in Kazakhstan. The Chechens' bombastic leader Jokhar Dudayev had been based in Estonia and witnessed the mass protests against the Soviet authorities there. He was also fully aware that his own Islamic credentials were weak and he thus infused much of his rhetoric with Islamic reference points. Dudayev appointed the Salafi-connected Islam Khalimov as his religious adviser, while his information campaign was organised by Movladi Udugov. The war had naturally intensified the religious element of Chechen identity and it proved a strong tool by which the resistance distinguished itself from the Russians. Coupled with a generational change in the resistance, this would create the propitious circumstances that eventually tipped the balance in favour of the Salafi component of the resistance leadership during the second war.

The Salafis helped facilitate an unusual alliance with a member of the Jordanian-Chechen diaspora community Fathi Mohammed Habib (aka Sheikh Ali Fathi al-Shishani) who arrived in Chechnya in 1993. Fathi was an elderly veteran of the jihad against the Soviets in Afghanistan and he began proselytising among Chechnya's youth with his small band of Jordanian-Chechen associates, soon amassing a group of around one hundred followers. Fathi was the most influential figure in establishing the foreign fighters' community in the North Caucasus in the early days.

Following Dudayev's assassination in April 1996, the poet and leading light of the failed Confederation of Mountain Peoples, Zelimkhan Yandarbiyev was appointed interim president of Chechnya's ruined de facto state. Yandarbiyev, who had recently grown a beard and adopted Islamic dress, immediately used his position to raise the prospect of a Chechnya under Shar'ia law and quickly enacted a new Criminal Code modelled on that of Sudan, signalling the beginning of the struggle between the nationalist and Islamist camps in the resistance.

In the post-Soviet era the identity of the Islamic population of Russia has not redefined itself as part of a broader identity group based around religion but has, in many places, maintained links with particular regional and sub-ethnic ethnic groups. These ethnic groups have continued to define themselves firstly as non-Russian rather than Islamic. Thus, the impact of religious identity is only part of the story of conflicts in Chechnya over the last three hundred years. It is also important to note that this tension did not commence with the collapse of the Soviet Union but that Chechen society and the Sufi Brotherhoods have long struggled to reconcile aspirations for Shar'ia law with local customary law, known as *adat*. Previous attempts to impose the Shar'ia by Chechen and Dagestani leaders of the *ghazavat*, or holy war, against the Russians have failed, though they still attained status as heroic, national figureheads.[25]

The source of the indigenous rivalry to the predominant Sufi Brotherhoods stemmed initially from those involved with the Islamic Renaissance Party (IRP). In June 1990, Akhmed Atayev, an elderly Dagestani who had lived in Tajikistan, established a branch of the All-Union IRP. Together with Islam Khalimov, a Chechen, and the Dagestani brothers Bagautdin and Abbas Kebedov they began facilitating links with Islamist groups in the Middle East. The IRP was ideologically aligned to the mainstream Sunni movements, the Muslim Brotherhood and the Pakistani Jama'at-i Islami. It relied on personal networks rather than formal organisational links though was instantly fragmented following the Soviet collapse.[26] A number of different strains of popular and intellectual Islam emerged from this, particularly in Dagestan, though all advocated the Islamisation of North Caucasian society with the ultimate aim of yoking the republics into a single imamate.[27]

A small support network of Arab financiers and facilitators had also emerged in the Caucasus following the brief war between Armenia and Azerbaijan over the Nagornyy-Karabakh enclave, with various charities supporting the Muslim refugee community.[28] These initial alliances between emerging indigenous Salafists in both Chechnya and Dagestan and their Middle Eastern counterparts at this critical historical juncture following the Soviet collapse was one of the key enablers that opened up the region to foreign fighters once the Russo-Chechen war erupted in December 1994.

Links between the North Caucasus and the Middle East are centuries old; Dagestan, for example, was once an important centre of Islam. Relations between the two regions have been shaped by Ottoman and Russian imperial policies, particularly the latter, which caused thousands of Chechens and other North Caucasians to migrate to modern day Turkey, Syria, Iraq and Jordan. While the Chechen Diaspora communities have been largely assimilated by the socio-political policies of Turkey, Syria and Iraq, there still exists a unique community of around 8,000 Jordanian-Chechens who have preserved their language and cultural traditions through time. Largely secular, the community is highly respected within Jordanian society and the country's politico-military elite.[29]

With de facto independence secured in 1996, the Chechens began searching for an organising principle for their new state-let, which included the status of Islam. In its new constitution, the independent Chechen Republic of Ichkeria was defined as Islamic, with little deliberation over what that actually entailed. Chechnya's first rebel President Jakhar Dudayev had represented the inherent tensions within Chechnya's resistance. Acutely aware of his poor Muslim credentials he increasingly adopted Islamic rhetoric as the conflict developed. He appointed Islam Khalimov, a doctor who was involved in establishing the original Islamic Renaissance Party in Chechnya, as one of his advisers. The Chechens also appointed Shamil Beno, a Jordanian Chechen, as foreign minister in order to raise awareness of their plight throughout the Middle East.

Trans-locality: actorness beyond the state

The effort to this point has been to outline a set of debates. My claim is that an important contribution to these debates can be made if we read violence as a phenomenon that is inscribed beyond the sovereign state. The corollary of this leads to an excavation of the interface between transnational institutions and the 'actorness' that such organisations display. Of course, this is not to say that cross-cultural identity and transnationalism are founded on similarity. Rather, the point is that these processes and forms of identity occur across political boundaries which may be inscribed culturally – they have some capacity, be it through agency or institutionalism, to influence political discourses as actors.

Here it is worth considering the work of Peter Mandaville, who is concerned with the way that boundaries and translocal identities are reproduced. For Mandaville it is not only culture, language, belief systems, memory and experience which generate forms of life and the power relations which inscribe them through identification with the nation, but that these differ from the techniques of governance associated with the state. States themselves are read as a product of a specific European, modern political culture which creates boundaries, temporal and spatial – such as the territorial nation-state – for the study of identities. But a translocal reading of culture sheds light on politics as 'a space of interaction situated across and between territories – interaction which is itself *constitutive of new political identities*'.[30] The notion of movement or of travel plays an important role in translocal accounts of identity. Mandaville notes that people and theories pass 'through translocalities, but they also travel *within* these spaces'.[31] So, arguably a translocal reading of identity affords the opportunity to explore both movement, as well as the complex multiplicity of subject positions. For instance, in parts of Europe peoples commonly moved, in today's parlance as 'economic migrants', in search of work. This created a distinct sub-group of people with common experiences – such as the *Gastarbeiter* community – who moved as guest workers to other parts of Europe.

When turning to identity formation, Iver Neumann argues that studies should focus on how boundaries 'come into existence and are maintained'.[32] While IR has traditionally recognized physical and economic borders,

Neumann draws attention to the processes through which 'social boundaries between human collectivities are maintained'.[33] Indeed Neumann argues that 'collective identities emerge as *multifaceted*, and must be studied as such'.[34] This serves to demonstrate why it is important to study the formation of armed resistance movements, to understand how they move from the periphery of collective identity groups, or vice-versa, how they get pushed out of collective identity groups, how they draw on cultural norms with a 'call to arms' and how they assimilate other causes when establishing a narrative. For example in Kosovo, the armed resistance movement remained small in number, clandestine, secretive and rural in character, whereas by 1999 in the North Caucasus, one wing of the anti-Russian movement, although focused on Chechnya, retained a regional political character. It seems to me that these processes have been challenged by the impact of globalisation, which has produced translocal readings of identity.

Translocality, according to Peter Mandaville, is an abstract space 'occupied by the sum and linkages *between* places (media, travel, import/export, etc). The notion of locality is included within the term in order to suggest a situatedness, but a situatedness which is never static. Translocality can be theorised as a mode, one which pertains not to how peoples and cultures exist *in* places, but rather how they move through them'.[35] Significantly then, Mandaville points towards the migratory practices which create political identity and the spaces which peoples and cultures occupy, along with their transformation through technological development and the processes of globalisation (media, travel, import/export). In this way translocal identity 'disrupts traditional constructions of political identity and gives rise to novel forms of political space'.[36] The emphasis here then is on the production of novel forms of political space, the groups which operate within them, and the social and cultural narratives which frame them.

Even though translocal identity does much to move beyond state-based notions of temporality and spatiality, and sheds light on the multiple processes of globalisation, highlighting the constitutive role of movement and technology, it still needs to draw on the political, cultural and historical narratives – as indicated in Chapters 1 and 2. This is important insofar as it illuminates the constitutive nature of social actors, in this case, as both insurgencies erupted in the Caucasus and the Balkans in the early 1990s.

Indeed, throughout the 1990s and within the broader economic, social and political framework of change between East and West, sections of the transforming Russian military began to refocus their aims and responses to emerging threats and separatist movements in the newly independent states of the former Soviet Union.[37] Significantly, as observers have illustrated, changes in the Russian political system since the end of Communism are, in

No estoy hecha para solucionar, solo para dilucidar.

El Dr. Magnus ha pensado y ha solucionado. Le disgustan realmente las depresiones. Supongo que la mía y la de otros pacientes. Le disturba que haya depresión en el mundo. Lo veo. Lo intuyo por su forma de escribir la receta. Con un bolígrafo que se asfixia en su mano. En mayúsculas. Contundente. Me viene una imagen ochentera a la cabeza: el Cazafantasmas de mi depresión, *Ghostbusters!* La preocupación por lo que escribe y diagnostica traspasa la cuadrícula oficial. Tinta malherida. Letra de psiquiatra luchador:

Venlafaxina, ayuda a Almudena.

No he realizado terapia hablada. No con un profesional. Un psicoterapeuta, una psicóloga, nada de nada. Tomar fármacos regulados ha sido mi medicina, la única. He conversado horas con Antonina, mi pareja, mi gato. Todo es terapia, recalcó el Dr. Magnus en una de nuestras sesiones: lo que has sacado de esto y lo que les has contado a los demás. Tu libro. Tu escritura. Tú misma, cambiando.

Al principio, en la consulta, apenas hablaba. Me sentaba en la esquina del sofá con un jersey grueso y Dr. Magnus lanzaba preguntas al aire dramático que se concentraba en la habitación. Por si contestaba a alguna. Hubo cuatro o cinco sesiones trágicas, indigestas, que me resultaron larguísimas, incluso él paraba la charla entrecortada y salía a buscar a mi tía, que se encontraba leyendo a oscuras, para calmar el tormento que se respiraba en el aire.

Un suspiro.

Con el paso de los meses, me fui curando. Al año de entrar en su consulta, ya comentábamos temas de actualidad, le envié los primeros capítulos de este libro y se desvivió en halagos. Aceptó ser el Dr. Magnus y en los correos electrónicos se empezó a despedir como tal: *Un abrazo, Dr. Magnus.* Congeniamos en cuanto a sentido del humor, complicidad tierna, respeto por Rafa Nadal, profundidad en las frases, sentimientos acelerados.

Sigo acudiendo a su consulta. Mi tía Antonina me acompaña y me empuja suave. Soy una persona con la fortaleza adecuada para pisotear el mundo. Estoy vitaminada con alegría: hemos disipado la ceniza que me asqueaba y me mataba lentamente. Y nos reímos en la consulta. En ocasiones me cuenta sucesos de su vida nada agradables. Otros son mejores. Y opinamos acerca de la rutina cotidiana: si nos gustan las navidades, jugar con los niños o me intereso acerca de su profesión.

¿Es muy duro aguantar la tristeza de los demás?

Nos intercambiamos los roles.

Es una amistad rara, medicinal.

part, linked to the military operation in Chechnya.[38] Thus, the manoeuvring of the Russian leadership in Moscow, keen to retain the geopolitical integrity of the Russian state, may be read as an attempt to inscribe political identity. But another dimension of this process is that the Russian military has some form of particular institutional and yet transnational 'actorness'. It is this capacity which is brought into sharp focus in Russo-Chechen relations as a combination of Russian military institutions has fought diverse elements of Chechen resistance.[39] Again, this calls into question not only the implications for political readings of identity, but also, of the 'actorness' of these organisations. Similarly, in keeping with attempts to reconfigure Russian domestic political identity, some groups used transnational networks or the support of NGOs to further the transformation of Russian politics.

Similarly in the case of the Balkans in the post-Cold War period, and more particularly the production of a Serbian narrative identity, we see how a number of events were 'negotiated in specific contexts' and 'strung together into one overarching story'.[40] The sense of plot – the unfolding of a series of events – helped to inscribe this process. The process of iteration, framed by notion of plot, helped to inscribe an emerging set of relations between self and other. However the reading of Kosovo as a frontier, replete with a host of histories and peoples, made it difficult to establish a single narrative to explain the complex relationship between groups originally assimilated in Yugoslavia and Albania. Moreover, the impact of Ottoman history and the role of an emerging myth of resistance, shaped by Albanian nationalism in the late nineteenth century, was compounded by religious differences which were 'transformed into ethnic and national antagonisms' throughout late nineteenth and twentieth century.[41]

Within the region, localised acts of insurrection and resistance perhaps typified by the *Kaçaks*, outlaws who had been active in Serb-controlled Kosovo throughout the 1920s, became commonplace. These groups drew on local support from clan and family members, established temporary regional coalitions, and operated throughout parts of Kosovo and its neighbouring environs. The enduring legacy of this period was the formation of Serbian and Albanian instantiations of national identity. However, Kosovo did not experience a national or even ethnic awakening, and only in the Communist period under Tito's rule did it experience limited autonomy in 1974 through Yugoslav constitutional change, and further reforms in the 1980s following the student riots in 1981. The period of Communist rule further polarised the communities in Kosovo, establishing geopolitical boundaries and borders which began to unravel and erode in the 1980s, following the death of Tito. By the early 1990s Kosovo itself was composed of a heterogeneous mix of peoples who had settled in rural hamlets and villages, with the capital, Pristina, largely inhabited by Serbs in central districts, surrounded by Albanian Kosovars living in the suburbs. The 1980s also witnessed a gradual economic decline throughout Yugoslavia which, in effect, exacerbated the rural–urban divide between the different groups in Kosovo. Tellingly, this local economic dynamic also helped to polarise the different groups in Kosovo along ethnic lines.

In both cases regional affiliates and Diaspora communities existed which travelled to the conflict zones throughout the 1990s. For instance by late 1998, the KLA benefited from the movement of peoples first to Albania and then Kosovo, and also due to the fact that a small but influential set of financial beneficiaries existed which sponsored the establishment of training camps. Meanwhile a large number of aid organisations quickly became involved in support of each conflict as post-Cold War international relations became shaped by trans-local readings of identity. In general then, the turn to translocal readings of identity within a broader international setting of late modernity, encapsulates a number of features which might include readings of technology, social mobility and the effects of globalisation. The first, the role of technology, has enabled more interconnections between groups, producing virtual and hybridised communities but it has, at the same time, also created ambivalence and insecurity within Western societies which rest heavily on specialised know-how, specialised institutions and processes. The second, mobility, was afforded to peoples as a result of social, cultural and economic changes. Conventional constraints, the family, employment, marriage were challenged in different ways, creating the conditions and opportunities for movement. The third, globalisation, intersects with the first two themes, producing different readings of identity.

Conclusion

Three broad points have been presented in this chapter: firstly, that the particularities of different identities are shaped by stories which draw together events and characters into a plot, identifying important, perhaps formative movements, when turning to national movements; secondly, that this process – in both Kosovo and Chechnya – differed considerably from the formation of Western European stories of ethnic and national identity, partly due to the differing bureaucratic processes of Communism – pressing together, perhaps even creating multiple and diffuse forms of identification; thirdly, that the narratives associated with ethnic identity in the Balkans and the Caucasus were neither fixed nor permanent but open to manipulation by strategists and politicians in the post-Cold War period. In other words, peoples were forced to adopt a single identity (Albanian/Serb/Croat/Slovene or Russian/

Chechen/Dagestani/Georgian) in peripheral regions where ethnic, national and religious forms of identification remained fluid and ambivalent. This, coupled with globalisation, created the conditions in which a sense of attachment, belonging and connectivity drew on incumbent, and yet unfinished national narratives.

This is exemplified by the anomalies we see emerging in this period, when external groups (Russia and Former Yugoslav Republics (FYR)) themselves sought to re-assert their identities. For example in the Caucasus we see the anomaly of the first Russo-Chechen War (1994–1996) – a war of separatism fought solely by the Chechens, a narrative of resistance produced at least in part by the suppression of rights and more particularly the Stalinist deportations of the Chechens and Ingush in 1944 – and as such, which differed considerably from the religiously motivated, multi-ethnic, anti-Russia guerrilla campaigns of earlier eras. In other words, insofar as this book is concerned, it is the modern totalitarian reaction to ethnic claims to succession throughout the later part of the 1980s and into the 1990s which provided one narrative, while founding events such as the deportations in Chechnya in 1944, and indeed the first war in Chechnya between 1994 and 1996, or the events in Kosovo in 1918 provide others. However, like the deportations in Chechnya in 1944, it was the events in 1960s Kosovo with the arrest and imprisonment of Adem Demaçi, the student uprising in 1981, and the gradual economic decline in Yugoslavia, which provided a link or living memory, and tied these earlier founding events into what Ricoeur calls a history of the present. This narrative link was deployed to mobilise groups, although it must be emphasised that these events and the ensuing narratives were also fractious – creating a multiplicity of competing groups – within the movements fighting against the Serb authorities and the Russian federal forces in 1999. Such divisions would of course inscribe the violence that occurred throughout 1998, as sub-groups who sought to develop different iterations of these founding events clashed. Similarly, the exploitation of networks of support for funding and recruitment and the use of Information Communication Technologies meant the movements formed, at least in part, as a result of the processes of globalisation: processes that were also impacting on the very idea of war.

Notes

1   N. Malcolm, *Kosovo: A Short History* (Macmillan: Basingstoke, 1998), p. 227. A *vilayet* is an Ottoman region of control.
2   *Ibid.*, p. 228.
3   *Ibid.*, pp. 234–235.

4   M. Vickers, *Between Serb and Albanian: A History of Kosovo* (London: Hurst & Co, 1998), p. 66.
5   *Ibid.*, p. 69.
6   *Ibid.*, p. 73
7   *Ibid.*, pp. 76–77.
8   *Ibid.*, p. 80.
9   *Ibid.*, p. 85.
10   Malcolm, *Kosovo*, p. 259.
11   S. Schwartz, '"Enverists" and "Titoists" – Communism and Islam in Albania and Kosova, 1941–99: From the Partisan Movement of the Second World War to the Kosova Liberation War', *The Journal of Communist Studies and Transition Politics*, Vol. 25, No. 1 (2009), p. 53.
12   *Ibid.*, p. 71.
13   Independent International Commission on Kosovo, *Kosovo Report* (Oxford: Oxford University Press, 2000), p. 35.
14   *Ibid.*, p. 36.
15   *Ibid.*, p. 37.
16   J. Hughes, 'Chechnya: The Causes of a Protracted Post-Soviet Conflict', *Civil Wars*, Vol. 4, No. 4 (2001), pp. 11–48.
17   G. Derlugian, *Bourdieu's Secret Admirer in the Caucasus: A World-System Biography (Chicago: University of Chicago Press, 2005)*, p. 237.
18   A. Jaimoukha, *The Circassians: A Handbook* (London: Routledge/Curzon, 2001), p. 85.
19   *Ibid.*, p. 85.
20   Derluguian, *Bourdieu's Secret Admirer*, p. 9.
21   T. de Waal, 'Basayev: Legendary Rebel Heroics', *The Moscow Times*, 20 June 1995.
22   C. Moore, 'The Tale of Ruslan Gelayev: Understanding the International Dimensions of the Chechen Wars', *Central Asia Caucasus Analyst*, Vol. 10, No. 10, available at: http://www.cacianalyst.org/?q=node/4868, accessed 10 January 2009.
23   C. Gall, 'Fighters Fall Back to Mountain Fortress', *The Independent*, 14 January 2005. See also Derlugian, *Bourdieu's Secret Admirer*, p. 60 and p. 237.
24   For a useful overview of the complex relations between the Chechens and Russians, and the differences within each respective group see B. Fowkes, 'Introduction', *Russia and Chechnia The Permanent Crisis: Essays on Russo-Chechen Relations* (Houndsmills: Macmillan Press, 1998), pp. 1–24.
25   M. Vachagayev, 'Chechen Society Today: Myths and Reality', *Central Asia and Caucasus*, Vol. 20, No. 2 (2003), pp. 1–9.
26   O. Roy, *The Foreign Policy of the Central Asian Islamic Renaissance Party* (New York: Council on Foreign Relations, 2000).
27   For a detailed survey of this phenomenon, see G. Yemelianova, 'Sufism and Politics in the North Caucasus', *Nationalities Papers*, Vol. 29, No. 4 (2001), pp. 661–688; A. Kudriavtsev, 'Wahhabism: Religious Extremism in the North Caucasus', *Central Asia and the Caucasus*, No. 3 (2000), pp. 131–137.
28   C. Moore and P. Tumelty, 'Foreign Fighters and the Case of Chechnya: A Critical Assessment', *Studies in Conflict and Terrorism*, Vol. 31, No. 5 (2008), pp. 412–433.
29   M. al-Shishani and C. Moore, 'Chechnya and Jordan: An Unquestioned Relationship',

Prague Watchdog., http://www.watchdog.cz/index.php?show=000000-000004-000003-000117&lang=1&bold=moore, accessed 24 July 2009. Estimates put the Chechen and Circassian Diaspora in Turkey at 100,000; Jordan, 8,000; Egypt, 5,000; Syria, 3,000; and Iraq, 2,500.

30 P. Mandaville, *Transnational Muslim Politics: Reimagining The Umma* (Routledge: London, 2002), p. 49.

31 P. Mandaville, 'When Meaning Travels: Muslim Translocality and the Politics of "Authenticity"', in A. Williams and P. Mandaville (eds.), *Meaning and International Relations* (London: Routledge, 2003), p. 119.

32 I. Neumann, 'Self and Other in International Relations', *European Journal of International Relations*, Vol. 2, No. 2 (1996), p. 167.

33 *Ibid.*

34 *Ibid.*

35 Mandaville, *Transnational Muslim Politics*, p. 50.

36 *Ibid.*

37 For example, the Russian military security service has transformed from the KGB to the FSK and in the mid-1990s to the FSB in an attempt to re-identify its own role in post-communist Russian politics.

38 A. Zelkina, 'The Chechen Future in the Russian Federation', *Helsinki Monitor*, No. 3 (2000), pp. 51–52.

39 A. Politkovskaya, *Novaya Gazeta*, No. 68 (16 September 2002), http://2002. novayagazeta. ru/nomer/2002/68n/n68n-s18.shtml.

40 I. Neumann, *Uses of the Other: 'The East' in European Identity Formation* (Minneapolis, MN: University of Minnesota Press, 1999), p. 218.

41 G. Duijzings, *Religion and the Politics of Identity in Kosovo* (Columbia: Columbia University Press, 2000), p. 29.

4

Globalisation and conflict: screening war in Kosovo and Chechnya

It may be argued that one of the defining features of contemporary world politics has been the alleged resurgence of insecurity as a source of different forms of war.[1] The end of the Cold War thus led to a reconsideration of questions of meaning in IR, alongside a broader set of debates about 'asymmetrical', 'fourth generation' and 'irregular warfare'. At around the same time the Gulf War issued in a consideration about the role of technology, gesturing toward a form of state-to-state conflict shaped by air-power and list-based targeting. However in the years immediately after the Gulf War, US strategy – which assumed, by 1992, an increasingly humanitarian and interventionist bent – was called into question in Somalia, while brutal conflicts erupted in the heart of Europe, in Bosnia, in Rwanda in Africa, in post-Soviet space in Georgia, in Nagornyy-Karabakh, in Tajikistan and latterly in Chechnya. The argument in this chapter – and for that matter this book as a whole – is that the end of the Cold War and the collapse of the Soviet Union did not simply signal a new era of war, but rather that these changes in global relations make it easier to see what has always been the case: that a hermeneutic approach is needed for the study of war IR.

In order to explore the contributions to debates about war within International Relations, this chapter begins with an appraisal of sorts which touches upon a more general critique of modernity as a way into understanding global politics.[2] In a general sense modern politics continues to valorise the state – even when diluted in the context of new waves of post-Cold War globalisation. Included within this general tendency are a number of characteristics such as the exclusive use of sovereign power by states, the control of their territories, distinctions between the 'domestic' and the 'foreign' as different, indeed separate realms, and the definition of distinct geopolitical boundaries. This way of seeing the international system is, of course, problematic, not least due to the increasingly differentiated forms of political identity, and indeed conflict, which question the way boundaries are inscribed.[3] Building on the last chapter, we turn here, firstly, to the two conditioning axes of compression and decompression as a way to understand postmodern war, before moving on to explore the hybridisation of war in the second part of the chapter. This section – subtitled 'screening war' – is drawn together in a concluding discussion of the 'picture economy'; the interface between media organisations, globalisation and the consumption of images and symbols. These distinctive features – and the processes afforded to them – played a crucial role, shaping the conflicts in the Balkans and the Caucasus.

Before developing these arguments, however, it is important to register precisely why a hermeneutic approach is needed so as to unlock or at least shed light on contemporary conflicts. In mainstream IR, conventional, conceptual and quantitative approaches largely focus on bombs and bullets, or strategies, elites and diplomacy, instead of on the meaning of the phenomenon of war, how it is understood by participants and how it is interpreted in different societies and cultures. Little research exists – in the mainstream at least – that focuses on specific events, how they occur, gain meaning and are described through language.[4] Evidently war is also about suffering, about images and symbols, and about identities, lived experiences and social life-worlds. The focus on narrative accounts of facts, events, texts or stories renders these aspects of war intelligible through interpretation, through hermeneutics. In other words, research needs to focus on language and on meanings. And research in IR needs to take into account the nature of texts and contexts, the different, indeed competing knowledge claims and conflict of interpretations, the intended audiences and background cultures against which questions render or elicit dialogue and generate meaning. Through hermeneutics – the human being – which is reflexive, which has an understanding of itself, the world and others, becomes the central focus of study. In particular the social life-worlds which contains within it shared meanings produced through dialogue, becomes amenable to hermeneutics.

For now though, we return to the central issue of this chapter; the changing nature of contemporary conflict.

The compression of conflict

In the broadest sense the processes of state formation – and the Westphalian system of sovereignty – included within it the compression of both identity through nationalism and the compression of the control of violence designed to face internal and external threats.[5] Thus the creation of the modern nation-state system storied war in a particular way, generating the idea of a police force and, eventually, a professional army. This process of compression was exacerbated by the emergence of political ideologies and the move towards modernisation. The first industrial conflict in which hundreds of thousands of peoples were killed by weapons that were mass-produced and manufactured in the forge of modernity – the American Civil War – provided an instantiation of this transformation in warfare. For Chris Coker the application of a 'scientific dynamic of the age' meant that war was no longer a 'test of character, a duel between warriors but a matter of impersonal calculation'.[6] Coker argues that three complex, interweaving aspects of human activity combine to produce war – the instrumental concept, the way war is applied by the state and the way it is viewed as rational instrument; the existential concept, how it is viewed by those who practice it (i.e. warriors or soldiers); and the metaphysical concept, insofar as war invests death with meaning.[7] The influence of technological change and modernity, for Coker at least, meant that war had become shaped by 'dis-enchantment'. Importantly though, Coker recognises how this process of change and the future of war may, in some quarters, be shaped by biotechnology, the 'technization' of the 'life world (including war), through instrumental reason' or, conversely by the 'sacrilizing of war, the privileging of the body over the spirit'.[8] In order to understand the future of war the answer for Coker is to walk the tightrope between these two positions, 'to make it sacred in terms of sacrifice, the willingness to die for a cause in which one believes', while also not surrendering war 'to computers with artificial intelligence who would feel no guilt, remorse for their actions or comprise the human dimension of war'.[9] It seems then, that the net effect of technology, modernity and industrialisation has been the compression of war, particularly in the West. However, the sense of industrial conflict enacted in the American Civil War masked another transformation, the emergence of political ideologies which would blight European politics and wars in the twentieth century.

The move established by the end of the European and Ottoman empires, combined with the emergence of political ideologies led some writers such as the Czech philosopher Jan Patočka to recognise that war in the twentieth century was shaped by a 'new techno-scientific age'.[10] According to Patočka, at the turn of the century the Western European military machine embodied a 'great sturdiness and persistence', but it also entertained a 'domineering rudeness and total absence of imagination'.[11] The forces unleashed in the 'techno-scientific age' – the shift from the First World War, to the Second World War and then the Cold War – meant that it was not a question of exploring wars of the twentieth century but rather to see the twentieth century 'as war'.[12] Again, the key driver was the rationalisation of war through compression. Albeit in different ways, the role of technological change has been raised in a series of theoretical sub-debates by the likes of Kalevi Holsti and Martin van Creveld.[13]

Others such as James Der Derian have brought the influence of the media and technology on conflict to the fore, highlighting what he labels 'virtual' war, in part drawing on Kosovo.[14] Drawing on Paul Virilio, Jean Baudrillard and Gilles Deleuze, Der Derian staked out a position that echoed much of the work in constructivist and postmodern IR theory. According to Der Derian, constructing a 'deterritorialized sense of being – neither here nor there as being but always as becoming different – virtuality represents a paradoxical extrareality that does not fit the dyad of the social sciences, the real and the ideal'.[15] He goes on to call this, 'virtual representation the *interzone*: neither realist nor idealist, utopian nor nihilist, but an interstice in which future possibilities are forged from the encounter between critical imagination and technological determinism'.[16] Clearly then, there are some overlaps with postmodern accounts of International Relations, and for that matter hyperreal or virtual studies of war.[17] Der Derian himself ponders whether the label postmodern would be apt, but ultimately opts for a broader reading of virtual theory, because of the admixture of imagination and technological determinism, and the role of mimesis and simulacra framed by the MIME-NET (Military–Industrial–Media–Entertainment Network). Elsewhere, Chris Hables Gray takes a similar line, focusing on the role of technology. In turn this pushes war into the realm of technology which may be useful when reading post-human conflict, but it does little to offer a reading of war not conditioned solely by this form of technological superiority. Nor does it shed light on the emergence of armed resistance movements within the context of globalisation. It is for these reasons that I break from both of these writers.

Nonetheless Der Derian, following Virilio, does point to the importance of another aspect of compression which is of interest here – that is the interface between war and its coverage through the news media. The Vietnam War, the first so-called 'televised war', demonstrated the then evolving connection between war and the media. It established a

> vital connection between what the world imposes and the mind demands, receives and reshapes ... In the Vietnam War what the soldiers and viewers saw on television made them question their own identity as Americans. In the past, the United States had never questioned that it embodied Western civilization, that its Asian enemies did not ... In Vietnam, civilization based on among other things, a high level of technological development was brought into question by the destructive potential of American technology.[18]

This is revealing insofar as it points towards a broader post-colonial discourse, while also exposing contemporary violence to processes of representation and reception, pushing conflict into a new televised age.[19] The result has been that some writers in IR have turned to an awareness of the visual aspects of security.[20] The supplementary impact of this process of compression meant that strategists, particularly those with a background in US military institutions, had a keen awareness of modern communications which fed directly into the first Gulf War.

In his book, *Waging Modern War: Bosnia, Kosovo and the Future of Combat,* Wesley Clarke reflects on the Bosnian conflict, noting that

> modern communications and the media – actions that were relatively small could have potentially large political impact, and therefore affect the course of an entire campaign. Such an incident occurred in the Gulf War, when our aircraft struck a command bunker that was being used as a bomb shelter by families. The lesson wasn't lost on us: watch the political impact of every decision and event.[21]

Clarke of course went on to devise the strategy for, and lead the NATO campaign in Kosovo, walking the tightrope of lessons learnt from the US experience in conflict, and marshalling the military requirements of a campaign supported by different European political and civil elites. He drew on his military experience to avoid the strategic problems faced by the US in another post-Cold War conflict 'to ensure that the military commander had the necessary legal authority to fulfil his limited and clearly specified responsibilities ... to avoid a repeat of Somalia'.[22] In short Clarke recognised that the strategic, tactical and operational levels of war 'had been compressed and their distinctions blurred' as a result of the local and international news media.[23]

Meanwhile others including Jean Baudrillard, and more significantly Paul Virilio, have long pointed to the idea of war as 'spectacle' shaped, in part, by the control of information as a key aspect of military confrontation.[24] These writers, and others such as Zlavoj Zizek, pointed to the compression of the local, international or global, through news media, and the resultant impact on war.[25] According to Virilio,

> [in] the Balkans, it was no longer a question of instituting a just war, but a legitimate or even a legalist war – war tailored to the interests of the world's last superpower and its absolute supremacy, particularly in the fields of satellite surveillance and information-gathering.[26]

Thus, the process of compression led to the establishment of new doctrines of war, which drew extensively on technological superiority.

The compression of war and technology, civil and military, politics and strategy – is however, accompanied by a change in the rhythm, cadence or speed of conflict. In some cases this led to protracted asymmetrical conflicts

– for example when Soviet forces invaded Afghanistan and fought the *muja-hideen*. Whereas other conflicts between states – such as the war over the Falkland Islands/Malvinas – occurred relatively quickly when compared with earlier campaigns. Even though many wars are asymmetrical, this did generate a burgeoning literature on the overlaps between civil conflicts and state-to-state military confrontations, a point raised again as the Cold War ended. But as Chapter 3 argued, the sense of compression did not stop with the end of the Cold War. Instead, this led to two aspects of compression: firstly, changes ushered in by technological change became intertwined with the responsibilities and actions of a host of international actors – from non-governmental organisations (NGOs) such as human rights groups, to international media groups and inter-governmental organisations (UN, NATO, OSCE). Secondly, US strategy became more entwined with some aspects of European politics. This contracted military and strategic aspects of conflict into the realm of politics, once again, blurring conventional boundaries associated with sovereign states.

The process of change reached a further stage in the wars in the Former Yugoslavia. The Balkan Wars of the early 1990s included an assortment of international actors (UN, EU, NATO, latterly the OSCE) and media organisations. The conflict was ended through international mediation, culminating in the Dayton Peace Accords. The influence was not focused on 'intervention' per se, but reflected a more visible awareness of conflicts, and a changing moral and legal international ecology which provided the milieu against which humanitarian intervention evolved. On the one hand then, the location of war may be changing, as conflict dynamics reflect and react to the changing international security environment. On the other hand, it seems that both Kosovo and Chechnya were fought through first order technology, missile strikes, the air superiority of the Russian army and NATO forces respectively, but also through militia and paramilitary groups, or the social networks of clans and families and Diaspora communities. In other words, these organisations and the conflict dynamics were also simultaneously impacted upon by the processes of decompression.

Decompression: post-national and post-humane war

One exponent of new wars, Mary Kaldor, illustrates that most wars that are localised 'involve a myriad of transnational connections so that the distinction between internal and external, between aggression (attacks from abroad) and repression (attacks from inside a country), or even between local and global are difficult to maintain'.[27] More recently Kaldor has noted that new wars take place in the context of failing states. They are fought by networks of state and non-state actors, where battles are rare and violence is directed mainly against civilians, and which are characterized by a new type of political economy involving a combination of extremist politics and criminality.[28]

The label Mary Kaldor used to describe the conflict in Bosnia (1992–1995) – which was at once civil, but shaped by internal and external forces, warlordism and criminality – was 'new wars'.[29] According to Kaldor, these types of conflict create large-scale civilian casualties, both through ethnic cleansing, but also because they are fought in civilian communities. This second point is of course, not new, given the war in Spain from 1936, or the US campaign in Vietnam. Indeed in the case of Vietnam, the war amongst the civilian population caused considerable policy problems, which would reverberate through the US military machine for many years thereafter. The more general problems associated with Kaldor's intervention, the lack of historical, empirical and contextual detail, have been raised elsewhere.[30]

Applying the label to describe the recent conflict in Iraq, Kaldor notes that this type of war needs to be 'analysed in terms of the disintegration of states and the changes in social relations under the impact of globalisation rather than in terms of technology'.[31] Two particular themes stand out in the work of Kaldor in relation to Bosnia; in one sense, although she does little to fully elaborate on the issue, the theme of criminal networks seems to offer an important way to move beyond the limitations of security in military terms alone, plugging into debates about social networks, insurgencies, militias, paramilitaries and warlords, and cultures, entrepreneurs or markets of violence.[32] Secondly, Kaldor's focus on globalisation as a way into reading political violence seems particularly pertinent, given the regional dimensions of conflict, the translocal reading of identity and the way that connectivities through globalisation allow Diaspora communities to play increasingly important roles in contemporary conflicts.

For another specialist, Mark Duffield, the idea of new wars or network war 'defines the global predicament. Across this contested landscape, bounded by the opportunities and threats afforded by globalization, new forms of autonomy, resistance and organized violence engage equally singular systems of international regulation, humanitarian intervention and social reconstruction.'[33] In this way, new wars are not centralised, nor solely determined by territoriality or hierarchical military and political structures, but are instead shaped by horizontal and networked groups which may plug into the emerging network of non-state actors. Even though Kaldor and Duffield introduced analysis to otherwise marginalised features of contemporary violence including the role of warlords, criminality, and issues of development and aid, it requires further integration into more recent alternative approaches to IR theory. That is to say, a form of IR, which is generally less dependent on states and political readings of nationalism, but still retains some of these features, may be useful, particularly when considering the social and cultural forces which shaped conflict in a globalising world. The result is a form of war that may be more readily understood as organised violence in a new era, differentiating it from inter-state war conducted between armies in distinct territories.

Albeit briefly, the intention here is to build on this work, and so address some of the aforementioned limitations in order to demonstrate why Kosovo and Chechnya may be considered as instantiations of postmodern war. It is worth making three points here: firstly, the processes which had shaped military institutions in Western Europe at least, tended to focus on hierarchical structures and frameworks. And yet as the burgeoning literature on networked war illustrated, globalisation meant that some conflict dynamics were shaped by flatter, or more horizontal forms of organisation, sometimes called networked or nomadic war.[34] The point here is not to labour attempts at re-inscribing control through techniques of governance, but instead, to draw attention to the interface between globalisation and local networks which help to inscribe forms of war, which governments are unable to shape or control. The reason for this is because the processes of globalisation – particularly those which create trans-local space – occur unevenly, but produce multiple, independent actors, and a plurality of audiences who act as conduits for information. This means it is essential to explore, examine and interpret cases in which media forms are questioned – for example the traditional broadcast media (television, broadsheet newspapers) and new media (online journals, YouTube) – or are traversed. In the words of David Kilcullen, whereas traditional media often focuses on small or local lifeworlds' – social networks 'allow enormous numbers of peoples to become consumers and producers of media content, shifting rapidly and seamlessly between these roles, sharing and producing information, and thus developing multiple sources of information, almost all of them outside of the control of governments and media corporations.'[35] Small media – for example audio tapes, pamphlets, and radio broadcasts – were themselves transformed as new technologies emerged.

Secondly then, even though de-centred groups have always played roles in insurgencies and guerrilla campaigns – the clash between these two themes – between the internal and external influences on war, might lead to novel forms of resistance or conflict dynamics not solely amenable to quantitative research.[36] Rather it is the process of blending, and the novel questions which arise that are of interest (i.e. how do external forces impact on insurgencies, what new international actors emerge, what of internal radicalisation within particular conflicts, and are insurgencies increasingly shaped not by imagery but by symbols?). In the case of both Kosovo and Chechnya, particular motifs rather than images alone, certain symbols and gestures rather than political manifestos or image-based representations have increasingly been used to create a sense of identification by groups involved in both conflicts.

The third and final point to draw attention to here, as a result of the unravelling of war, refers to the different actors themselves. Globalisation, coupled with the end of the Cold War released the pressure on war, freeing it from its common points of reference throughout the twentieth century – the nation, the state, and political ideology – and investing it with new and old constituent parts.[37] One implication of this process was the ability of actors to relay information and (re)present war in different locations, locally and globally, but another is that other actors operate in different political spaces with warlords being at one end of a large spectrum of actors with, for instance, human rights organisations at the other. How then, do post-colonial campaigns combine with anti-globalisation movements, and how does this shape a new international security ecology? The interface between these actors, their ability to shape the international security ecology, and their interconnection with traditional, local and mythic stories of war, creates multiple competing narratives.

The unravelling of traditional modes of conflict, combined with its recompression in some contexts has led to an alternative form of contemporary violence which can be called postmodern war. Arguably, this differs significantly from many of the examples discussed so far, insomuch as it places emphasis on the ability of war to be apprehended, captured and storied in new ways.

Hybridity: conflict in post-Communist space

By the late 1980s a doctrinal shift occurred in some sections of the US military machine – framing the use of force as a tool of humanitarian intervention.[38] This led the US to embark on an unprecedented range of military missions; including the invasion of Panama in 1989 to capture General Noriega, and led the allied operations in the first Gulf War in 1991. The momentum from these military interventions caused the US to send 30,000 troops to Somalia in 1992, to intervene and act on behalf of the international community, to ensure the safe delivery of aid, and to use humanitarian intervention without the risk of involvement in protracted conflicts. At the same time the processes linked to the decompression of conflicts, the use of paramilitary, private or contract soldiers, mercenaries, militias and volunteers, often linked to political authorities but also enmeshed in local socio-economic, clan, tribal and criminal networks, became more commonplace. As Pertti Joenniemi notes, this was not necessarily new, however 'what was previously viewed as excessive and seen as constituting a relatively unimportant residue in regard to the way modern war was unfolding has, more recently, and unexpectedly gained ground'.[39] What was once exceptional – wars between states – is now considered normal, whereas what was unconventional – irregular conflicts – now dominate contemporary international politics.

Alongside this conceptual inversion, the impact of globalisation and mass communications has gone some way to produce an alternative form of conflict which draws on 'pre-modern structures and ideologies', but which is shaped by 'new technology' including 'communications and media tools'.[40] Although focusing on the US, and the idea of insurgency and counter-terrorism post-9/11, the military strategist David Kilcullen nonetheless calls this type of conflict 'hybrid warfare'. These conflicts combine 'new actors with new technology and new or transfigured ways of war, but the old threats remain and have to be dealt with at the same time in the same space, stressing the resources and overloading of Western militaries'.[41] For Kilcullen, hybridity is shaped by a different threat environment increasingly interpenetrated by globalisation. For the most part, I agree, but the focus here is to take a step back, to locate, understand and interpret the conflicts in Kosovo and Chechnya – in the context of a slightly different post-Cold War security ecology.

One reason for doing so is to place the conflicts in Kosovo and Chechnya in the trajectory of strategic, political and military change highlighted by Kilcullen and others, while also retaining an awareness of the then nascent features of the wave of globalisation which impacted on these conflicts as they unfolded in 1998. By focusing on the diverse groups involved in each armed struggle (the KLA and the radical and moderate wings of the Chechen resistance), another is to draw attention to particular features of both cases, against the backdrop of the break-up of Socialist Yugoslavia and the dissolution of the USSR. However, to echo the note of caution raised by some commentators who have sought to highlight 'illogical parallels' when considering the conflicts in Kosovo and Chechnya; it is extremely difficult to develop comparative studies of the two cases due to the unique characteristics tied into each example.[42] Notwithstanding this note of caution, others have highlighted that the wars in Kosovo and Chechnya were fashioned by a shared system of 'ethno-federalism'; that is, the USSR and Yugoslavia were asymmetrical federations which 'consisted of territorial units with different status'.[43] At the same time, the two conflicts were 'framed and shaped by the administrative-territorial borders of crumbling empires'.[44] There are numerous offshoots of this process of hybridisation, particularly when war is screened, when images, motifs and symbols alone are used to articulate a narrative, and when these narratives are interpenetrated by 'the picture economy'.

Screening war: the picture economy

The idea of screening war, much like the ideas of compression and decompression, is used here to point towards the Janus-faced role of the image media. In one sense, this refers to the process of showing and representing wars – that is, the display and projection of images – while also drawing attention to the processes designed to curtail and cut off, separate and conceal, or to protect and guard against the circulation of imagery related to war. Walter Benjamin, in a piece entitled 'The Work of Art in the Age of Mechanical Reproduction', argued that the domain of the visual had been transformed by the processes of reproduction, which now placed imagery in the realm of 'another practice – politics'.[45] One reason for this was the acceleration of the processes of reproduction; another was the interface with an economy which, when tied to the reproduction of the pictorial and located within the processes of contemporary globalisation, generates a new politicised realm: the 'picture economy'.

The 'picture economy' – be it in the use of visuals, symbols and imagery by the state or resistance movements – is of course framed in different ways. It has been transformed further by its explicit usage as part of campaigns of propaganda, which are themselves enveloped in changes associated with globalisation. Not only has this led to the increasing importance of the media through its assorted network reach, different means of communication, and increasing importance of associated institutions, it has, according to Elaine Scarry, led to less deliberation and consent within Western populations which are now 'infantilized and marginalized'.[46] Although the focus of Scarry's critique lies in the depiction and reception of war in the Western world, this does point towards another challenging trend in which insurgencies turn to the use of symbols and local images (of, for instance, massacres) in order to further their cause.[47] This is particularly interesting because memory, according to some psychologists, largely draws on a visual record of events.[48] This may provide some evidence of the impact of visual images, pictures, photographs and symbols on studies of insurgencies – particularly insofar as insurgents seek to use and control the 'picture economy'.

Meanwhile, the picture economy might include the filming of brutal and savage attacks, creating a kind of war-pornography – souvenirs as part of 'trophy collecting in war' – but which can be circulated through an informal market economy.[49] Many of these 'snuff videos' serve typical local and personal combat narratives – victory against the odds, emphasising the weakness of the enemy, evidence of mass slaughter, pride in shedding blood – but these are co-joined with broader stories of epic resistance and tragedy.[50] The visceral nature of such images are designed to cause excitement, highlight the assertiveness of the self, or indeed, to glorify actions or shame victims, in effect dis-inhibiting the viewer to acts of extreme violence in war. However, such images may also be used for recruitment, to romanticise particular conflicts or even to highlight war crimes. The co-mingling of imagery and sounds presents an alternative representation of war that operates through different channels and is extremely difficult to counter.

Chechnya, Kosovo and the picture economy

Chechen groups have been at the forefront of the use of imagery as part of their respective war and terror campaigns. Movladi Udugov, a spin-doctor in the first Chechen War (1994–1996), pioneered the use of satellite technology to allow US news channels to conduct 'live' interviews with Jokhar Dudayev, the then leader of the Chechen resistance. Udugov, Ibn Khattab (the leader of the Arab *mujahideen* in Chechnya) and Shamil Basayev all became adept at using many forms of imagery, pioneering the filming of attacks for pay or to raise funds for their cause through the sale of graphic videos and DVDs.[51] Even though groups such as the Liberation Tigers of Tamil Eelam or Hezbollah (and more recently Hamas) have a long history of using media imagery, Chechnya has a unique position in the development of information war, the 'cottage-industry' of producing, copying and distributing videos, DVDs and CDs representing elements of the Chechen resistance, the use of web-feeds and web-pages which link the Chechen cause with other conflicts, and the way that transnational networks have employed such tools for the recruitment of foreign fighters.[52]

At the same time, the cultural dissemination of identity through an interconnected network of channels including radio, television and more recently through the Internet in streamed videos provides an alternative translocal source of identity affirmation. Indeed, while the videos and imagery continue to present a veneer of political control the content of this 'unofficial identity' captures characteristics that may be culturally defined. Such videos reveal a subtle shift towards alternative networks of identity in which imagery and sounds reference general geographical areas, with troops and militias which have different visual commonalities, such as beards, or allegiances to other sub-state groups, rather than uniforms and equipment which differentiate them from an enemy. In the first Chechen War separatist fighters often wore green headbands inscribed with Koranic verse to demonstrate international

Islamic solidarity. This emphasis on the connections between the culture and conflict invites viewers to identify with both elements. Of course another reason for this use of video imagery may well be the capturing of evidence of acts in order to secure funds and support from benefactors.

However, at the same time, other pressures from outside the region also did much to create a picture economy which impacted upon the second war in Chechnya. This had its history in the impact of the end of Communist rule in Russia, the burgeoning influence of the media in the first war, and the more general globalisation of news which occurred throughout the 1990s. As if to highlight the creeping influence of an image economy on the conflict, rather aptly we turn here to the words of the award-winning Czech journalist, Petra Prochazkova in the documentary *Chechen Lullaby*. She says

As a journalist who comes and goes, you don't get it.

I have been filming this war for many years; from around December '94.

I was trying to capture the images of the war, the explosions, because that was what they wanted. These were the pictures they wanted. The more bodies the better, the more blood the better.

That's how it went on for many years …

After the first war, when they exhumed the bodies, I went to film them. It is amazing how many people were buried there.

Now things are even worse. But now, no one is looking for graves …

I began to think, is this all that is left of a man after death, just a pair of boots?

I was filming these corpses and thinking to myself, that's a great image, in the foreground you have got these huge new boots, and behind them all that is left of a man.

Sort of a strange symbol.

People were always coming with me to help me film, and they would ask, how is this going to help you or us, they will see it in Europe and then what?

To be honest, I didn't feel sorry for those people. And I doubt that any journalists felt sorry for them; what they want is pictures, or something to write about. Maybe later they will feel a little sorry, but first, they want to do their job. I was the same.

Then, last September, I was filming with the Russians in Dagestan; when the APC I was on, hit a mine.

I often remember the conversation I had with my bosses at Czech TV. I get through to them and say, I just got blown up on a mine and my camera was running, to which they reply, 'excellent'. Well I had been expecting them to say something like, are you alright or, was anyone killed?

Actually, someone was killed.

I remember them dragging him out, and what was left of his legs, slipping on the APC. And there was a sound like a wet fish being pulled out of something; dreadful sound. There was a trail of blood; they weren't legs any more, but rags. He died right there. I filmed his last breath. That taught me something terrible.

I feel pity for people when they die before your eyes. But, on the other hand, the journalist inside you is telling you, these people would have died anyway, so it is just good it happened in front of your camera. But you know, if you start to think like that it is the end. That's when I knew I had to stop. The longer this war has gone on …

The idea that I am doing something really important, that I can stop this war by filming it, it is just not true.

In other words a third strand or interface links international public consumption to a wave of globalisation. In this sense it is the 'freedom to consume images rather than the freedom to shape the reality behind the images'.[53] The last chapter drew attention to this process by illustrating how identities were mediated by translocality. It is this combination which produces a 'picture economy' which operates as part of, what Paul Virilio calls the 'fourth estate'.[54]

Reflecting on the latter point in relation to the war in Bosnia, the Croat writer Dubravka Ugresic repeated a story she had heard. Following an attack a TV reporter in an unnamed Bosnian hamlet paid the surviving members of a village to 'drag the scattered corpses into a tidy heap so he could photograph them. At the same time he did not quite grasp either where he was, or who was who, and he made a moving TV commentary about the Muslim massacre of Serbs. The corpses were Muslim.'[55] Whether true or not, the point of the story is to draw attention to the economy which contrives to refashion the use of pictures by the media; Carol Midgley, the then *Times* media correspondent, offered a telling reflection on this process following a decision by the BBC not to broadcast images from Kosovo. Midgley notes that

technology, such as the 'home video' evidence of mass killings provided by the KLA, has given news chiefs access to a vast array of explicit images of atrocities. Horrific footage that showed the bloodied faces of dead ethnic Albanians contorted in agony was cut from the BBC's Six O'Clock News seconds before it went on air. The executive editor of the BBC television news said, 'We see some gruesome stuff which you could never show on television … You have a duty to tell the news how it is, to get the real story across without offending people.'[56]

Thus, while the Serbs retained a tight control of the media, which NATO forces tried to 'degrade' in the war in 1999, the KLA also adopted a distinctive information campaign (using news bulletins, hosting a website) as part of its broader strategic goals; the KLA's aim was to trigger international intervention by the international community.[57] Alastair Campbell, the chief British political spin-doctor, recognised that the Kosovan campaign presented a qualitatively different form of war. Campbell indicates, 'in this changed media environment, in a modern conflict, particularly one fought by an Alliance of nations, with different politics, different military systems and different histories, effective communication is not merely a legitimate function; it is an essential one.[58] Of course, as Mark Pedelty notes, different audiences certainly have the capacity to interpret and redefine media imagery. 'Nevertheless, as long as people are functioning primarily as "consumers", critical or otherwise, they are still lending their support and social power to the dominant system, consumer capitalism.'[59]

However, the vacuum afforded by the end of Communism shaped the consumer space in different ways; in Russia and Serbia, in the Caucasus and the Balkans. While Russia witnessed an exponential growth in media outlets throughout the 1990s, the latter part of the decade saw these independent media corporations become more centralised and politicised, as Putin's Kremlin exerted pressure on independent media. In Serbia, the media remained under the control of the political elite in Belgrade.

Conclusion

This chapter has demonstrated overlaps between those who focus on technology as a way into postmodern war and others who focus on new and late-modern conflict. It has sought to retain the label postmodern war – to point to the processes of hybridisation and the movement towards the spaces and interfaces between compression and decompression when considering contemporary conflicts. These two forces, along with the interface between mythic and news accounts of war have interpenetrated contemporary conflict.

This locates postmodern war between the over-determined readings of virtual and Western war and the work on new wars which, to some extent, lacks effective historical or epistemological contextualisation. This chapter provides analysis of two cases and the contexts of meanings which shape contemporary violence in Kosovo and Chechnya. This is, of course, why the term postmodern war is used here, as a movement beyond modernism, in the strategy, form and reality of war, and also in its epistemological and ontological sense of meaning developed in the first few chapters of this book. That is to say that conventional approaches to war in IR focus on strategies, salvoes and shells, and not language and meaning, which is precisely why a hermeneutic form of research is needed to interpret the complexities of contemporary violence. War then, has to be submitted to a richer, inclusive array of theoretical and practical forms of analyses, placing it more readily as a problem of interpretation for hermeneutics. Hermeneutics, especially the branches linked to stories, to narratives, to meaning and interpretation, shines light on the excitement and outpouring of emotion, the dark, grotesque and yet beautiful aspects of conflict, the strange perversions and attractiveness associated with battle, which together impact on culture, which dominates political and personal memory, which transforms language and which gives life meaning. War brings into sharp relief not only questions of meaning though; it exposes IR to richer conceptual readings of conflict and to the meaning of violence itself.

Notes

1   A representative sample of work within and outside of IR might include P. Wallensteen and K. Axell, 'Conflict Resolution and the End of the Cold War, 1989–93', *Journal of Peace Research*, Vol. 31, No. 3 (1994), pp. 333–349; M. Shaw, *Post-Military Society: Militarism, Demilitarization and War at the End of the Twentieth Century* (Cambridge: Polity Press, 1991); J. Koehler and C. Zürcher (eds.), *Potentials of Disorder* (Manchester: Manchester University Press, 2003).

2   Amongst others, this point is articulated in some of the work of Rob Walker. See R.B.J. Walker, *Inside/Outside: International Relations as Political Theory* (Cambridge: Cambridge University Press, 1993), p. 18.

3   Some of these theoretical points are touched upon in a theoretical appraisal of humanitarian or 'late modern' war by Vivienne Jabri. See her *War and the Transformation of Global Politics* (London: Palgrave, 2007).

4   Of course within the literature on social constructivism and critical security studies, there does exist some research that focuses on the role of language and meaning in conflicts. See for example, Karin M. Fierke, 'Multiple Identities, Interfacing Games: The Social Construction of Western Action in Bosnia', *European Journal of International Relations*, Vol. 2, No. 4 (1996), pp. 467–497 and Karin M. Fierke, *Changing Games, Changing Strategies* (Manchester: Manchester University Press, 1998). Although the question of how language describes the realities of conflict and war more generally is beyond the scope of this book, it is worth noting that many of those I have interviewed who have participated in the conflicts in Kosovo and Chechnya are rarely concerned with language per se, given that they have actually fought or suffered in war. Much of the meaning of war for my interviewees was described in largely emotional terms, using language which would rarely be found in theoretical books on mainstream IR.

5   B. Anderson, *Imagined Communities* (London: Verso, 1991).

6   C. Coker, *The Future of War: The Re-Enchantment of War in the Twenty-First Century* (Oxford: Blackwell Publishing, 2004), p. 3.

7   *Ibid.*, p. 6.

8   *Ibid.*, p. 142.

9   *Ibid.*

10 J. Patočka, *Heretical Essays in the Philosophy of History* (Open Court: Chicago, 1996), p. 122.

11 *Ibid.*, p. 123.

12 *Ibid.*, pp. 119–137.

13 K. Holsti, *The State, War, and the State of War* (Cambridge: Cambridge University Press, 1996); M. van Creveld, *The Transformation of War* (New York: Free Press, 1991).

14   J. Der Derian, *Virtuous War: Mapping the Military-Industrial-Media-Entertainment Network* (Boulder, CO: Westview Press, 2001), particularly Chapter 8. Others such as Michael Ignatieff have used the label 'Virtual War' to describe the conflict in Kosovo, but this is more of a rehashing of the works of Baudrillard, rather than an argument per se. M. Ignatieff, *Virtual War: Kosovo and Beyond* (London: Chatto & Windus, 2000).

15   Der Derian, *Virtuous War*, p. 211.

16   *Ibid.*

17   Even though others have employed the term hyperreal war, it is often attributed to, and has been used by Donna Harraway. See Chris Hables Gray, *Post-Modern War: The New Politics of Conflict* (London: Routledge, 1997), p. 21.

18   C. Coker, 'Post-Modernity and the End of the Cold War: Has War been Disinvented?', *Review of International Studies*, Vol. 18 (1992), p. 197.

19   For an excellent discussion of the role of television in relation to the war in Kosovo see Andreas Benhke 'vvv.nato.int. Virtuousness, Virtuality, and Virtuosity in NATO's Representation of the Kosovo Campaign', in S. Medvedev and P. van Ham (eds.), *Mapping European Security after Kosovo* (Manchester: Manchester University Press, 2002), pp. 126–144.

20   Beyond those mentioned in this chapter, interventions associated with poststructural writers such as Michael Shapiro, 'Strategic Discourse/Discursive Strategy: The Representation of 'Security Policy' in the Video Age', *International Studies Quarterly*, Vol. 34, No. 3 (1990), pp. 327–340, or by scholars of Critical Security Studies (CSS) including Michael C. Williams, 'Words, Images, Enemies: Securitization and International Politics', *International Studies Quarterly*, Vol. 47, No. 4 (2003), pp. 511–531 have touched on aspects of security and imagery. However within feminist/poststructural work (Laura Shepherd; Lene Hansen), those involved in the turn to cultural texts (Jutta Weldes; Iver Neumann) and more recently, those leading the 'aesthetic turn' (Roland Bleiker) have been at the forefront of exploring visual aspects of security. Indeed it seems to me that the three latter groups of work mentioned here are leading the way exploring visual, pictorial and image-based accounts of IR and security, while of course, outside of IR others have made significant interventions.

21   W. Clarke, *Waging Modern War: Bosnia, Kosovo and the Future of Combat* (New York: Public Affairs, 2001), pp. 85–86.

22   *Ibid.*, p. 59.

23   *Ibid.*, p. 86.

24   J. Baudrillard, *The Gulf War Did Not Take Place* (Sydney: Power Publications, 1995); Paul Virilio, *War and Cinema: The Logistics of Perception* (London: Verso, 1990).

25   Z. Žižek, *Welcome to the Desert of the Real* (New York: Verso, 2002).

26   P. Virilio (2000) *From Modernism to Hypermodernism* (London: Sage, 2000), p. 70.

27   M. Kaldor, *New and Old Wars: Organized Violence in a New Era* (Cambridge: Polity Press, 1999), pp. 1–2.

28   M. Kaldor, 'The "New War" in Iraq', *Theoria*, Vol. 53, No. 109 (2006), p. 1.

29   Kaldor, *New and Old Wars*.

30   E. Newman, 'The "New Wars" Debate: A Historical Perspective is Needed', *Security*

Dialogue, Vol. 35, No. 2 (2004), pp. 173–189; Erik Melander, Magnus Öberg and Jonathan Hall, 'Are 'New Wars' More Atrocious? Battle Severity, Civilians Killed and Forced Migration Before and After the End of the Cold War', *European Journal of International Relations*, Vol. 15, No. 3 (2009), pp. 505–536.

31 Kaldor, 'The "New War" in Iraq', p. 1.

32 E. Kohlman, *Al-Qaida's Jihad in Europe: The Afghan-Bosnian Network* (Oxford: Berg, 2004).

33 M. Duffield, 'War as a Network Enterprise: The New Security Terrain and its Implications', *Cultural Values*, Vol. 6, No. 1–2 (2002), p. 153.

34 For the former on networked war, see J. Arquilla and D. Rondfeldt, 'Cyberwar is Coming!', *Journal of Comparative Strategy*, Vol. 12, No. 2 (1993), pp. 141–165 and for the latter on nomadism, see J. Reid, 'Deleuze's War Machine: Nomadism Against the State', *Millennium: Journal of International Studies*, Vol. 32, No. 1 (2003), pp. 57–85.

35 D. Kilcullen, *The Accidental Guerrilla: Fighting Small Wars in the Midst of a Big One* (London: Hurst & Co, 2009), p. 11.

36 The reference to quantitative studies is used to draw attention to one version of work associated with Paul Collier that fixes accounts of war dynamics firmly within quantitative accounts of globalisation. This approach is more commonly known as the greed versus grievance or the Collier–Hoeffler model. For example see P. Collier, A. Hoeffler and M. Söderbom, 'On the Duration of Civil War', *Journal of Peace Research*, Vol. 41, No. 3 (2004), pp. 253–273.

37 P. Joenniemi, 'Toward the End of War? Peeking Through the Gap', *Alternatives*, Vol. 33 (2008), pp. 233–148.

38 L. Freedman, 'Escalators and Quagmires: Expectations and the Use of Force', *International Affairs*, Vol. 67, No. 1 (1992), pp. 15–31.

39 Joenniemi, 'Toward the End of War?', p. 244.

40 Kilcullen, *The Accidental Guerrilla*, p. 6.

41 *Ibid.*, pp. 5–6.

42 E. Stepanova, 'Kosovo and Chechnya: Illogical Parallels', *Security Dialogue*, Vol. 31, No. 1 (2000), pp. 135–137.

43 Koehler and Zürcher, *Potentials of Disorder*, p. 4.

44 *Ibid.*, p. 4.

45 W. Benjamin, 'The Work of Art in the Age of Mechanical Reproduction', *Illuminations* (Pimlico: London, 1999), p. 218.

46 E. Scarry, 'Watching and Authorizing the Gulf War', in M. Garber, J. Matlock and R. Walkowitz (eds.), *Media Spectacles* (London: Routledge, 1993), p. 59.

47 I am indebted to Neville Bolt for raising this point in a private conversation in 2009.

48 And on this point I am indebted to Andrew Hoskins. He noted that one leading psychologist, Martin Conway, speaking at a 'Memory and War' forum in December 2008 claimed that '85% of our memories contain visual images', in personal correspondence in 2009.

49 This serves to move debate beyond the insights highlighted by the likes of J. Bourke, *An Intimate History of Killing: Face-to-Face Killing in Twentieth-Century Warfare* (London: Granta, 1999), pp. 13–43, or the magisterial work by E. Scarry, *The Body*

in Pain: The Making and Unmaking of the World (Oxford: Oxford University Press, 1995).

50 Bourke, *Intimate History of Killing*, pp. 37–43.

51 G. Derluguian, *Bourdieu's Secret Admirer in the Caucasus: A World Systems Biography* (Chicago: Chicago University Press, 2005), pp. 41–43.

52 C. Moore and P. Tumelty, 'Foreign Fighters and the Case of Chechnya: A Critical Assessment', *Studies in Conflict and Terrorism*, Vol. 31, No. 5 (2008), pp. 412–433; C. Moore and P. Tumelty, 'Assessing Unholy Alliances in Chechnya: From Communism and Nationalism, to Islamism and Salafism', *The Journal of Communist Studies and Transitions Politics*, Vol. 25, No. 1 (2009), pp. 73–94 .

53 R. Anderson, 'The Ideological Significance of New Photography: The Case of El Salvador', *Ideologies and Literature*, Vol. 3, No. 2 (1988), p. 245. cited in Pedelty, *War Stories: The Culture of the Foreign Correspondents* (London: Routledge, 1995), p. 14.

54 For a broad discussion of this aspect of the media, see P. Virilio, trans. Julie Rose, *The Art of the Motor* (Minneapolis, MN: University of Minnesota Press, 1995).

55 D. Urgesic, 'The Culture of Lies', *Index on Censorship*, Vol. 23, May/June (1994), p. 40.

56 C. Midgley, 'TV News Dilemma Over Torture Images', *The Times*, 19 June 1999.

57 P. Neumann and M.L.R. Smith, *The Strategy of Terrorism: How it Works, and Why it Fails* (Routledge: London, 2008), p. 40.

58 A. Campbell, 'Communications Lessons for NATO, the Military and Media', *The RUSI Journal*, Vol. 144, Issue 4 (1999), pp. 31–36.

59 Pedelty, *War Stories*, p. 14.

5

Stories of war in the Balkans and Caucasus

A substantial amount of theoretical literature now exists in both International Relations and political theory which explores how culture impacts upon violence. As yet, however, this body of literature has not been applied fully to analyse the move to war in either Kosovo or Chechnya.[1] Aside from exploring the cultural construction of an enemy – enemification – and locating this within a broader body of work on colonialism and post-colonialism, this chapter argues that stories play an important role straddling the divide between culture and politics. In many ways stories interpenetrate these two realms – aided, as mentioned in Chapter 4, by the advent of the 'picture economy'. Stories can be found in both myths and also in literature, and this chapter will explore how these narratives are formed, how they shape conflict and how they gave war meaning in Kosovo and Chechnya. In order to highlight the processes of interpenetration here, we turn to the issue of heroic stories, grounded in myths, which helped to polarise the Serbian and Russian sense of collective identity, and generate a narrative of resistance in Kosovo and Chechnya.

The chapter begins by re-visiting ideas of narrative and plot, drawing attention to the role of epic stories. The second part of the chapter explores these ideas in relation to the rise to power of Slobodan Milosević and the production of a Serbian sense of victimhood. Along with the centralised control of the media, these themes combined in an epic story arc, which focused on Kosovo, ultimately leading to the emergence of an armed resistance movement. The third part of the chapter explores these ideas in relation to culture and empire in Russia, plotting the moves which led to the transformation of the armed resistance movement in Chechnya. In particular, this section sheds light on the ways in which the idea of an enemy is constructed, often drawing on literary sources and stories. The final section of the chapter seeks to explore how a domestic threat is often popularised, and which, through stereotypes is used to produce a homogenous image of an internal enemy. However, by the late 1990s a complex mix of groups, formed around shifting alliances, became involved in anti-Russian resistance, and this ultimately led to two different phases of suicide attacks. The first phase of suicide attacks were conflict-related, tactical and were largely orchestrated by groups associated, locally at least, with factions who had long opposed Maskhadov's presidency. These groups, although they had pledged to resist a Russian incursion, fought for a multiplicity of reasons. They were explicitly targeted in the initial stages of the second war by federal authorities, while the second phase of suicide terrorism between December 2002 and September 2004 were organised and conducted by Chechens and pro-Chechen sub-ethnic groups operating under a broader long-term agenda of pan-Caucasian anti-Russian resistance. In other words, analysis of violence should consider the cultural context in which the idea of an enemy is produced and inscribed.

Marshalling stories: narratives and identity

As already argued, analyses of war can be enriched through the study of stories and narrative – particularly through the use of plot. As Ricoeur argues, 'the specific model of the interconnection of events constituted by emplotment allows us to integrate with permanence in time what seems to be its contrary in the domain of same-ness identity, namely diversity, variability, discontinuity, and instability'.[2] Identity, when understood at the level of emplotment, can be 'described in dynamic terms by the competition between demand for the concordance and the admission of discordances which, up to the close of the story, threaten this identity'.[3] Emplotment then, sheds light on the act of composition, how the process of story-making mediates between concordance and discordance. In this way, as Erik Ringmar argues, narrative calls attention to how meanings are 'inserted into the context of our lives'.[4] The key then, for Ringmar at least, is to demonstrate how experiences and memories come together in narratives, how they are associated with particular words, meanings and contexts, or how they reverberate. Crucially though, this process also gives rise to '*collective* experiences and *shared* memories which give rise to reverberations that are held in common by large groups of people'.[5] In order to demarcate the limits of these stories about identity, political elites draw on histories – fact and fiction – and then project identity claims through the prism of narrative onto audiences; the reaction of the audience then leads to recognition, legitimacy and, in some cases the endorsement of authority.

Political elites turn to recognisable stories such as epics and tragedies, precisely because they are recognisable and easy to consume. While there is a burgeoning field on the latter in IR, the former provides a useful hook for re-interpreting events in the Balkans in the 1990s.[6] Epics – often written in what is called an 'elevated style' and captured in poetic verse – aim to retell the story or exploits of superhuman heroes. The heroes often represent a specific group, and capture the traits and wills of a particular community. The story itself refers to the journey through mysterious, fantastic or cosmic lands. During the journey the hero in the story often undertakes deeds. On occasion the hero is helped by Gods, or other supernatural beings, often in unforeseen ways. Yet, as one writer has noted when considering Serbian folkloric tales, epic 'poems are not merely entertaining stories of legendary or historical heroes, they summarize and express the nature or ideal of an entire nation at a significant or crucial period of its history'.[7] In fact the 'characteristics of the hero' in epics 'are national rather than individual, and the exercise of those traits in heroic deeds serves to glorify a sense of national pride. The epic hero triumphs over evils – real or imaginary – which are those most feared by the people of a region or nation that he represents'.[8] Notwithstanding the gender bias and somewhat problematic reading of epic and history in the work of Koljević, features of this mode of story-telling are nonetheless helpful. The epic not only demonstrates a series of overlaps with the story of the nation, but also helps to establish boundaries, produce fears and insecurities, and capture emotions and moments of glory. The more recent, what may be called critical analyses of epics, highlight how they rest in studies of genre, produce complex histories and generate complicated fields of interpretation.[9]

Here then it may be useful to turn to an example – from Greek literature – to help flesh out some of these features which are of use for my analysis. Even though different versions of the story exist, the journey of Jason and the Argonauts provides a useful example here. Jason and his companions on the Argo undertake a journey in search of the Golden Fleece. In this example, during the journey the hero – Jason – travels through mysterious realms, performing superhuman deeds sometimes with the help of the Gods.[10] The reason for drawing attention to the epic story of Jason and the Argonauts is to illustrate the role of story and the importance of different forms of story-telling. The former – the story – provides an arc which links a set of deeds or events, thereby locating characters in the narrative. The latter – that is the epic form of the tale – draws attention to the narration, the ability to mix fact and fiction. Together the story arc of the epic generates meaning – it is a way of apprehending a set of events, capturing the characters and illustrating the transmutation of the hero. Jason, a young, somewhat naive man, learns a set of skills, demonstrates leadership during the story, and eventually changes through the journey itself.

While epic forms of story-telling may appear far removed from IR, the world of international relations is in fact embedded within, and replete with the traces of this form of narrative; be it in rituals, ceremonies and/or the monuments erected to evoke a sense of belonging and emotional attachment to a region or locale. As Anthony D. Smith notes, rather than imagination 'the communion of the nation is one that is felt, willed and acted out in the real world'.[11] The idea of the epic, a popular, readily digestible story arc, helps to plot events in a broader narrative, in this case about the rise and decline of the Serbian empire. In many ways the issue of rebirth transmuted the former Communist party member Slobodan Milosević into a nationalist; providing a significant role in the turn to war in Kosovo. At the same time, the story of Serbia and Kosovo moved attention away from the gradual economic decline of Yugoslavia as a whole under Communism, to one of competing post-Communist national identities. A subsidiary aim of the act of story-telling is to evoke an emotional sense of connection or belonging. This is important, because it sheds light not only on suffering as a motive or driver for action, but also on the projection of salvation and rebirth, which propels narrative and drives actions.[12] In other words, the idea of the comparison with the character of epics is useful because it points to the story arc – the way in which events are produced, acted out and portrayed.

The story of Serbia and Kosovo

As already demonstrated, a number of national identities formed in the nineteenth and twentieth centuries which would have an impact on Kosovar secessionist claims in 1999. The most notable were those claims made about Serbian and Albanian national identity, although others including Macedonian and Croatian identity claims would also play an important role in the region, when turning to the conflicts in Bosnia and Kosovo respectively. Meanwhile the decline of empires, particularly the Ottoman Empire, and the rise of a post-Second World War model of Yugoslavia created another politicised layer, which added to the contestation of identity claims. The contested nature of identity, and the borders which frame identity claims, mean that groups on the periphery of empires experience a process which produces multiple and changing affiliations. As anthropologists and sociologists have demonstrated, these claims are themselves plural, and may be more effectively understood as 'belonging' or 'connectedness', so as to demonstrate the emotional attachment to a region, place and context – that is, identity may be situational – while also overlapping with other claims of identification, based on other things including gender, class, sexuality, or ethnicity.[13]

When mapped onto the Balkans this serves to highlight the importance of Kosovo in the establishment of a sense of Serbian national identity, even if the processes of narrative configuration ironed-out the discordant elements of the story. According to Noel Malcolm the 'Kosovo myth', communicated through the folk-poetic tradition, 'supplied the essence of a special type of historical-national self-consciousness for the Serbs', but this was 'a product of the nineteenth century'.[14] It was, as Malcolm notes, a product of national-ist writers and nation-builders, including Vuk Karadžić and Petar Petrović Njegoš, who transformed the myth into a national ideology.[15] The reason for doing so is not surprising, given that ideas of nationalism were developing across many parts of Europe, which in Serbia's case 'involved the idea of rebelling against, or making war on, the Ottoman Turks. A national myth centring on the symbolic moment of Turkish conquest both focused atten-tion on the enemy, and reminded Serbs of a glorious pre-Ottoman past'.[16]

Similar rhetorical manoeuvres and motifs were deployed by some of the Serbian political elite in the mid-1980s and the 1990s, as Yugoslavia disin-tegrated. The process of narrative transmutation fashioned by elements of the Serbian political elite occurred over a period of seven or eight years, following the death of Tito in 1980. The process was twofold, producing and constituting both an identity for the 'self' and for the 'other', while also taping into tropes linked to myth. Importantly, as Peter Levi notes, 'Lazar's choice between Turkish vassalage and honourable death in battle is seen here as the dilemma between the earthly and the heavenly kingdom, which is, in fact, an echo from Serbian medieval literature.'[17] Embracing the idea of narrative transmutation Milosević, and for that matter other Balkan leaders, shifted from Communist Party members to saviours of the nation, serving a higher cause, sacrificing their lives – echoing the choice of Prince Lazar – in the service of national identity.

This can also be broken down into a number of recognisable stories; Serbian suffering at the hands of Kosovar Albanians, salvation through the establishment of a cult or mythic leader, both of which are easily identifiable in epic stories. Furthermore, this also aligned the collective identity of the Serbian peoples with commonly-held ideas about religious identity, embrac-ing the role of the Church in the immediate post-Cold War years. In turn this fed into the story advanced by Milosević, which in many ways, mirrored parables – short narratives designed to demonstrate moral authority.

National re-Birth and the Milosević era: from Yugoslavia to Serbia

A number of events occurred in the story of Milosević's rise to power, many of which were linked to Kosovo. These events occurred against the backdrop of post-Tito Yugoslavia, providing a key element in the emergence of a unifying narrative about Serbia, and also in stories about the cultural construction of an enemy. Firstly, a series of petitions – each gaining more support – were circulated in 1982, 1985 and 1986 demanding action over the status of Serbs in Kosovo. These were accompanied by public demonstrations prompting popular dissent directed against Kosovar Albanians. Meanwhile work by 'prominent academics' from the Serbian Academy of Sciences and Arts – on what became known as the *Memorandum* – sparked intellectual debate about the status of the Serb population in Yugoslavia. It illustrated

> that the Serbs were discriminated against by Yugoslavia's constitutional structure. It pointed out that 24 per cent of Serbs lived outside Serbia while 40.3 per cent lived outside the boundaries of central Serbia, that is to say either outside Serbia itself or in Kosovo and Vojvodina. Part of the rationale of giving power to Serbia's provinces had been that otherwise Serbia, by far the most populous republic … would inevitably dominate the rest of Yugoslavia, and thus provoke an anti-Serb and anti-Yugoslav reaction. Now the policy was beginning to rebound.[18]

Moreover the language of the *Memorandum* exacerbated its impact. It asserted that 'The physical, political, legal, and cultural genocide of the Serbian population of Kosovo and Metohija is a worse historical defeat than any experienced in the liberation wars waged by Serbia from the Serbian Uprising in 1804 to the uprising of 1941.'[19] Lastly, it evoked a sense of meaning through the process of injuring, drawing not only on the idea of Serbian suffering and victimhood, but also propelling the narrative forward through the connection between ancient and recent history – the yoke of which had burdened Serbia since 1389.

One element in the story of Serbia under Milosević was the narration of events by political elites through the prism of the epic. This was used in order to flag up the need for the rebirth of the nation, built on ethnic difference. In order to latch onto this theme the Serb political elite, and indeed media organisations, drew on the widespread reportage of incidents which highlighted injustice and Albanian or Kosovar violence directed against Serbs or Christians. The first of these, the death of a Serb soldier in 1987, became well known as a result of Serbian coverage. As the journalist Tim Judah notes, 'On the 3 September Aziz Kelmendi, an Albanian conscript in the army, went berserk, killing four other conscripts before turning the gun on himself. Only one was Serb, but the Serbian media, which was increasingly coming under Milosevic's influence and control, unleashed a barrage of anti-Albanian venom, describing the act of this deranged individual as a pre-meditated Albanian separatist attack.'[20] The way the deaths were reported evoked a sense of difference, subtly suggesting that the attack was the product of Albanian nationalism. Another case, an attack on a nun in 1982 who 'was allegedly beaten up and raped by ethnic Albanian youths', served to highlight religious differences between communities in Yugoslavia.[21] The story evoked a sense that the 'other' – the Albanian population in Yugoslavia – were barbaric.

A final case, an alleged attack on a Serb from Kosovo in May 1985 – echoed this theme, citing Albanians as the perpetrators of the attack. However, it was also the nature of the injury which was tellingly manipulated by Serb nationalists. The Serb farmer – Djordje Martinović – entered hospital having had a bottle forced into his rectum. This echoed the use of impalement by the Turkish Viziers under Ottoman rule.[22] Here it might be well to inject a specific example, drawing on the literary work of Ivo Andrić in his magisterial book *The Bridge Over the Drina*. The opening chapters of the book retell the story of the bridge being built in Bosnia, under the orders of the Ottoman Vizier. But the building is systematically sabotaged by people from the local community. After a lengthy search, one of the saboteurs is captured and tortured, culminating in his impalement. Andrić writes, 'From a distance it could be guessed that the stake to which his legs had been bound at the ankles passed right through his body … He was alive and conscious. His ribs rose and fell, the veins in his neck pulsed and his eyes kept turning unceasingly. Through the clenched teeth came a long drawn-out groaning in which a few words could with difficulty be distinguished. "Turks, Turks …" moaned the man on the stake, "Turks on the bridge … may you die like dogs … like dogs."'[23] As Julie Mertus notes in her book *Kosovo: How Myths and Truths Started a War*, linking the Martinović case 'with an impaling and Kosovo Albanians with Ottoman Turks had an enormous impact on Serbian consciousness … The impalement metaphor worked well to further feelings of endangerment and to propel the desire for historical revenge.'[24] Thus, the powerful cocktail of myths and media coverage helped to demarcate religious, ethnic and racial boundaries. This fed into the idea of national rebirth, itself tied into the story of the Field of Blackbirds in 1389. In turn, this enabled the cultural construction of an enemy: the Kosovar Albanians.

Mertus goes on to argue that the 'people of the region … pattern their behaviour around what *they* believe to be true, based not on what some outside "expert" writes but on their own personal experiences and on the myths perpetuated by the local media and other popular storytellers.'[25] In essence therefore, Serbian politicians used the myth of Serbian victimhood to tap into a groundswell of emotions about national identity. These were intimately linked to the status of Kosovo, and the position of the Serbian community within it. Increasingly the language of difference was used to present the case, in one sense as a clash between different 'ethnic' groups (Serbs and Albanians/Kosovans) and in another, as a problem which undermined the very idea of the federal system of rule in Yugoslavia. The *Memorandum* was one aspect of this story, linking then current concerns with a powerful myth about the downfall of the Serbian empire as referenced in the work of Vuk Karadžić. However, this process also served to construct, through culture, the image of a barbarian 'other', a group which were more savage and less civilised than the Serbian elite.

By May 1989 in a party *coup de grâce*, Slobodan Milosević replaced his mentor and the former President of Serbia, Ivan Stambolić. This move paved the way for the transformation of Milosević from a Communist apparatchik to a nationalist leader, and ultimately to the status, for some, of a Serbian hero. In 1989, Slobodan Milosević organised a 'million-man march' to celebrate the anniversary of the Battle of Kosovo in 1389. However, it was multi-party elections around a year after the 'million man march' which signalled a growing divide over the status of Kosovo. The newly formed Serbian Socialist party won considerable support. In this period of transition, new laws were introduced disadvantaging the status of the Albanian population in Kosovo, with a constitutional amendment which revoked the autonomy of the region, which was passed in 1990.

Four further elements of the Serbian narrative of identity embraced by Milosević were collapsed into the broader plot. These framed events throughout the latter part of the 1980s and into the 1990s.

1   the issue of Kosovo was deemed a product of Serbian nationalist tendencies which reached their nadir in the mid-1990s in the wars in Bosnia. This does much to underplay the role of other national elites, particularly in Croatia, in the disintegration of Yugoslavia. This also downplays the general economic decline in Yugoslavia throughout the 1980s;

2   the story arc places responsibility for the actions of the disintegration of the former Yugoslavia – in the Serb narrative marshalled by Milosević – firmly in the orbit of external groups, and particularly the European states that recognised Slovene and Croat calls for secession from Serbian-controlled Yugoslavia. In a sense, however, this serves to re-affirm the third point, and yet also underplays the role of the first point;

3   the focus on political elites neglects the popularisation of myths and the connections between particular issues related to belonging. The depiction – in stories, rituals or through images – of identity is often replaced

with mantras and widely held motifs about the Balkans as a 'tinderbox' or site of ancient hatred;

4   chronology is disrupted by the plot – in one sense, suggesting that the events in Kosovo were a product of events in Bosnia, rather than recognising that the Kosovo myth predated – and provided the very foundation for the transformation of Milosević from Communist to nationalist. In another sense, the chronology of events are emploted providing a narrative arc, linking the 'defeat' in Kosovo in 1389 with the re-establishment of post-Communist Serbian identity claims in 1989.

As noted in Chapter 4, the important point is to recognise how these points, particularly points 2 and 4, fed into the nature of the conflict which erupted in Kosovo in the 1990s. Chapter 7 will expand on some of these ideas further. Neveretheless, the corollary of this process of emplotment about Kosovo not only helped to generate the idea of ethnic conflict in Kosovo, it also had two further effects when considering the character of the war in 1999: firstly, it firmly located the issue of Kosovo as an internal issue, meaning the conflict would involve not only the Serbian army, but also more specifically Serbian police, and an internal armed resistance movement, the KLA. By 1999 they would be joined by a variety of other actors, including NATO, involved in 'humanitarian' intervention; NGOs, the OSCE and the EU. Secondly, the narrative embraced by Milosević also created cleavages within the Kosovar Albanian community; some advocating passive resistance, others opting for armed confrontation eventually leading to the creation of the KLA. Similar cleavages also played a role in creating moderates and radicals involved in the Russo-Chechen War which erupted in 1999. But before exploring them, it is important to consider the linkages between culture and the imagination of empire, when turning to Russia and the North Caucasus. Thereafter this chapter will turn, albeit briefly, to explore how a complex and competing set of narratives and groups (both from within, but also from outside of Chechnya) that were involved in the anti-Russian resistance were homogenised into one radical, Islamic and bandit enemy that posed a domestic threat to the idea of a resurgent Russia.

Culture and the imagination of empire

One only has to read the short stories of Russian literary greats such as Tolstoy to recognise the complex range of ethnic groups in the Caucasus which have often caused problems for the Russian political elite based in Moscow. Thus the Russian literature of empire and writings of the likes of Pushkin identify that 'territorial boundaries and political allegiances were marked by deeper forms of cultural and ethnic solidarity'.[26] In other words, war continued to be perceived as a modern political tool understood in direct relation to threats to the integrity of the Western form of political organisation – the state – and to the sovereignty and homogeneity of political identity embodied in the nation-state. Clearly this has implications for the analysis of contemporary violence. When assessing the Russo-Chechen conflicts of the 1800s a similar theme of identity contestation comes to the fore. Tolstoy's last classic, *Hadji Murat*,[27] offers a way into interrogating Russo-Chechen violence in a 'different light'.[28] The book demonstrates that a tension exists between a politicised and European modern discourse of war and a version of violence which appears alien to that discourse.

Cultural interfaces can condition violence, and the transformation of violence highlighted by some writers may further expand the analysis of contemporary violence. Reading violence in this way illustrates how cultural expressions of meaning, evoked in stories, often use the notion of threat, and particularly the threat to empire, as a way of bolstering discourses of identity. The production of political meaning or imagination of empire may, therefore, operate through a system of signs which excludes and encodes meaning.[29] The cultural specificity of literature is of interest here. In 1907, as Russia reacted to new threats (Japan), the breakdown of empire and the transformation of war, the poetry of Belyi provided insight into the apocalyptic threat to Russian cultural identity.

> It is necessary to understand that the red dragon hurtling towards us from the East is illusory: these are misty clouds and not reality; there is really no war at all; it is a product of our morbid imagination, an external symbol in the struggle of the universal soul with the universal horror, the symbol of the struggle of our souls with the chimeras and hydras of chaos.[30]

This evocation of a morbid nightmare, an imaginary apocalyptic foe and thus a symbolic struggle echoes the reading of de-territorial technologised violence in the work of Der Derian. As if to mirror the threat to the Russian empire, the Watson Institute symposium demonstrated how apocalypse was used as a threat to the cultural identity of the United States after 11 September 2001.[31] In doing so, the symposium showed how threat to empire is born out of metaphorical identification of global fear. The narration states: 'The old mythic terror, the apocalypse, has been revived and fortified by computer projections. There are those who now say the human race won't make it through the century.' The poetry of Belyi and the work of the Information–Technology–War–Peace programme intersect and become not only a major source of cultural insight but also a vehicle for interpreting the manifold cultural aspects of empire. In this way, war becomes a cultural spectacle and literature may be used to identify the various 'structures of resistance' and the 'systematised' institutional and political practices which inform the cultural dimensions of violence. In this sense, by concentrating on the politico-cultural dimensions of war, hermeneutic readings point to the ontology of experience. As a result of this hermeneutic approach meaning manifests itself in communication, in culturally constituted traditions often played out in literature.

Internal dissent and Russo-Chechen violence

In studies of literature and empire, scholars have tended to highlight the role that literary accounts play in constructing internal political identity through encounter. One way in which writers have sought to further their insight is through the role of different genres. Genres, or types of story, offer a way into reading the contradictions of identity. They can, for example, highlight the role of the personal or they may offer insight into the complex relationship between the natural and modern world played out in romantic representations of the 'other'. Both Marklinsky's *Ammalat Bek* and Tolstoy's *Hadji Murat* demonstrate the contradictions of Russo-Chechen storytelling.[32] As Susan Layton points out, literature relating to Russo-Chechen relations may capture the inconsistencies of modern political identity and empire. Layton notes that Pushkin's correspondence in the 1820s used the term Circassian which encompassed 'an all-purpose name for mountaineers' but paid particular attention to 'Chechens as especially war devoted people'.[33] Yet, as the violence escalated in the 1830s, Russian 'pulp' literature began to re-characterise the mountaineer or highlander as a 'vicious woman-beating thug' whose actions were organised around blood feuds and vendettas.

Here, this body of literature reflects a transformation in the representation of the 'other' as a direct result of the Russian campaign against the highlanders of the Caucasus. This point is, once again, mirrored in the shift between the public perceptions of the Chechens throughout the two campaigns of the 1990s.[34] Similarly, it also becomes possible to understand how Russian identity, played out in the Caucasus, has been constructed around colonial narratives and a romantic vision of encounter. 'A romantic myth quickly developed … combining the artist's need to flee the suffocating constraints of civilisation and a paradoxical awareness that this path to freedom had first to be cleared by the tsar's armies.'[35] There are, however, different ways of reading this colonial and post-colonial heritage which complement political representations of recent histories. The emergence of common messages in romantic and colonial literature afforded, for example, the cultural construction of a 'noble savage'; a Caucasian hills-man.

Nevertheless, the cultural construction of the 'noble savage' also identified de-political forces which affect resistance. As scholars have noted, for the noble savage 'life cannot generate an ideologically coherent message … revolt is both too personal and too universal; in either case its politics are thereby muted'.[36] Thus, in the case of Russo-Chechen relations, the writer, the artist and the poet offer overlapping discourses of identity. Tolstoy in his short stories, or Lermontov and the genre of romantic poems exhibit a capacity to tell stories. In other words, through genre they offer insight into the 'ontology of the moving subject'.[37] Storytelling is therefore a means of expressing internal dissent and capturing contested identity. One facet of this process derives from the contradictions of internal dissent within a state. In the Russo-Chechen case the cultural construction of a noble savage has been brought into sharp focus. In the Russian poetry of empire, the 'artist thus became an ambiguous third element in the otherwise binary conflict between the colonizer and the colonized … most Russian writers … finally chose both options: hence the difficulty of ascribing a single political meaning to their work'.[38] Thus, literature does not necessarily have either a coherent or a uniform political message. Yet literature offers insight into internal cultural dissent. In this way literature is a culturally specific messenger of sorts. It can be used to explore contested political identities because it presents a destabilised sense of cultural identity which permeates violent relations. Marlinsky, author of the *Ammalat Bek*, created a 'Dagestani hero as both Islamic other and surrogate self'.[39] In *Ammalat Bek*, Marlinsky points to the Chechen as an 'Asiatic enemy' and yet he repeats 'the hearsay that Gazi-Muhammed [a Chechen imam] was the grandson of a Russian turncoat – the offspring of anti-tsarist sentiment in the readership's own country'.[40] In short, literature identified the cultural nodes of identity inscription encoded in violent encounters beyond the state.

Similarly, as commentators have noted, the savage 'other' was an attraction for the Russian elite because 'as a primitive he was closer to nature, while his ferocious opposition to Russian rule elevated sympathy as a prism through which to contemplate the however limited creative resistances of the Russian poets to his own political system'.[41] The tension between the Russian authority as empire (in either tsarist or Soviet form) and the new discourse of dissent associated with groups working in opposition to the state (media moguls and oligarchs) offers a way of reading the internal dissent associated with contemporary wars. Still further, some literature also echoes the facets of violence identified by theorists of 'new wars'; the 'paramilitaries, warlords, militias and transnational organisations' which condition contemporary violence.

In this sense, literary insight can be political, but literature also provides social, cultural and historical functions which are especially important when analyses turn to the interpretation of the encounter between different political communities. Thus, we see in much of historical literature – for instance in the work of Tolstoy – an awareness that Russian political culture restricts direct political commentary. Russian literary culture has had to function 'privately and later, furtively, as it tried to cope with indifference, underdeveloped taste and state censorship'.[42] As if to emphasise this point, different accounts of Russian political identity have traversed a succession of forms of Russian political identity – tsarist, Soviet and post-communist – which has lacked a means of direct internal political dissent. So we can see how examples of literature which focus on Russo-Chechen relations captured a distinctive character in Russian literary history.

As different forms of writing became popular, the ability to write and reproduce the written word mirrored the political encounter in the Caucasus. In this way it can be said that Russian literature offers a means to convey a certain political and cultural uniformity which gains a further sense of coherence when compared with the mountainous, tribal and clan structures of the Chechen peoples. Likewise, one can make a further claim illustrating how literature gives insight into understanding some practical characteristics of war. For example, looting and the use of contract soldiers, mercenaries and paid fighters have long been recognised as intrinsic facets of the Russian war-fighting machine.[43] In a short interchange in *The Raid* the institutionalised nature of the actions of such groups are highlighted. "'Well, how about it, Colonel?" said the general. "Let them loot, I see they are terribly anxious to" he added with a smile, pointing at the Cossacks.'[44]

In contrast, other sections of the Russian military machine and the actual practice of the fighting have been conditioned by the use of contract soldiers (*kontrakniki*). Much like the Cossack mercenaries in Tolstoy's story, these troops serve as part of the Russian army on a contractual basis. However, a further point is, as if to echo *The Cossacks* mentioned in *The Raid*, that these 'contract' soldiers were involved in looting throughout Chechnya.[45] The use of Russian literature, then, illustrates two points for IR theory. The first, simply, is that identity is constructed through culture and often captures the manifold messages associated with violence and internal dissent. The second is that identity played out in culture is not fixed spatially. In other words, as we have seen, literature demonstrates that meaning may be contextualised. In short, the meaning of one's own identity and that of the 'other' oscillates and is shaped through culturally organised dissent and encounter.

One war, many wars: territoriality, domestic space and enemification

Throughout the early 1990s, successful separatism in Chechnya not only raised concerns in Moscow regarding potential breakaway republics within the Russian federation but it also highlighted the challenge to the single politico-cultural identity emanating from the state's bounded territorial space.[46] In the 1990s it had become commonplace in the Russian domestic media to present Chechen separatism in stereotypical cultural forms – 'the Russian professional soldier faces the Chechen bandit'.[47] In light of this, interpreting the containment of the domestic 'other' in the first Russo-Chechen campaign can be read as an attempt to reconfigure a singular politico-cultural identity of Russia. Indeed, the expurgation of the domestic – the 'us' – and the extirpation of the foreign – the 'other' – can be seen as an attempt to constitute political identity by expelling 'from the resultant "domestic" space ... all that comes to be regarded as alien, foreign and dangerous'.[48] Violence is, therefore, reproduced and played out in different domains through dissimilar practices.[49] As Human Rights Watch Reports indicate, in 'a disturbing new trend, Russian forces increasingly resort to blowing up the bodies of executed Chechens – a crude ploy that eradicates signs of torture, obscures the cause of death, and makes identification of the corpse extremely difficult'.[50] This indicates how the meaning of violence may be shaped through the cultural construction of an enemy.

One particular dimension of this process which requires further analysis is the cultural reproduction and cultural stereotyping of violent identities or what can be called 'enemification'. Two points can be made here. In one sense, the popular stereotype of the Chechen as a noble highlander was manipulated first into a bandit and into an Islamic terrorist.[51] In another sense, atrocities against both Russian and Chechen civilians become excluded in a two-way process in which the political inscribes the cultural and then, thereafter, through which politico-cultural identity is absolutised. Enemification occurs in protracted violence through cultural stereotyping, but although it is formed in accordance with political identities it is disseminated through the cultural classification of 'us' and 'other'. One important aspect of this process derives from the representation of acts of violence, including the commemoration of atrocity. Here we see a very different reaction, for example, to female suicide attacks in Sri Lanka, Israel – Palestine and Chechnya.

In the case of Chechnya numerous attacks have been committed by men, and particularly by members of the Nogay sub-ethnic community. Furthermore, suicide attacks occurred in at least two phases – the first orchestrated by the Barayev and Akhmadov loyalists (June 2000–October 2002), and the second as part of Basayev's Operation Boomerang (December

2002–September 2004). However, popular accounts of this phenomenon in international news coverage, and even some academic commentaries, tend to misread Chechen suicide attacks, often conflating isolated and unsanctioned acts of revenge (such as the Moscow Metro suicide attacks in February 2004) with the tactical use of suicide operations, misreading complex intergroup dynamics, mixing mass hostage-taking with suicide attacks, in order to quantify the phenomenon. This produces a simple, digestible motif: of the barbarous Chechen Islamic 'other'; replete with a kingpin – Shamil Basayev – directing the attacks by a group of vengeful female suicide bombers called 'black widows'. For now though, the argument here is that the analysis of violence is forced to consider the cultural context in which the idea of an enemy is reproduced: the structures which prejudice identities and the interplays which reconstruct and mediate identity.

The corollary of this attempt to erase the domestic threat of Chechen identity is played out in the numerous accounts of unmarked graves.[52] Moreover, the practice of undermining identity through disappearances or masking attacks further complicates this issue and yet it also becomes intelligible.[53] In this way, the use of balaclavas by Russian forces, or attempts to remove identification tags on clothing, or number plates on vehicles when conducting *Zachistka* (sweep) operations is not only a tactical issue but can be seen as part of an attempt to undermine the cultural and psychological status of the Chechen population in Russia. Indeed, some commentators have argued that it has been a 'war of representations' with the contestation over the control of 'representation' providing an altogether different front line.[54] In the second Russo-Chechen campaign, the ability of the Russian government to 'absolutise' the conflict in Chechnya is of considerable importance. On the one hand, by presenting Chechens as Islamic terrorists they therefore become a component of the war on international terror.[55] On the other hand, this may also be read as an attempt to consolidate the image of the Chechens as the enemy within – who take up arms to oppose the policies designed to re-establish Russian identity. This further polarises the cultural identities in the conflict itself.

Conclusion

In order to explore the use of narrative here, we turned firstly to a reconsideration of different forms of story, highlighting the use of the epic as a way to understand the journey of Serbia from Yugoslavia to a post-Communist state. The idea of stories are useful – particularly when turning to the Balkans and North Caucasus – because each are not only areas in which multiple groups live, but the locales themselves and the sense of belonging within them, are contested. In other words the two regions are often referenced in literature, in its many forms – and myth (oral histories, folkloric tales, songs, legends) – which goes some way to capture the contestation between identity claims, and the tensions and ambiguities inherent within them.[56] Competing identity claims and contested borders within the Caucasus and Balkans were complicated further; firstly by the federal policies under Communist rule; secondly, as demonstrated in Chapter 3 because these regions – and Kosovo and Chechnya within them – have historically been on the periphery of empires; thirdly, because the legitimacy and authority of the political elites in Belgrade and Moscow were intimately involved in the production of stories – stories which established different ethnic and religious tropes – through culture; and finally, because part of the process of narration by the centre required a mix of the visual and written, and factual and fictive tropes in order to plug into common story arcs and genres such as epics. In both cases, stories were used to help construct the image of an enemy, drawing on cultural sources. This process, here called enemification, provides a point of departure for further study. Nonetheless in this chapter, it serves to provide a way into re-reading the violence that erupted in post-Communist states in the 1990s, especially when tied to globalisation and the hybridity of war – generating another layer in the international security ecology.

Notes

1   Notable exceptions to this general rule exist. See V. Tishkov, *Chechnya: Life in a War-Torn Society* (Berkeley, CA: University of California Press, 2004).
2   P. Ricoeur, *Oneself As Another* (Chicago: University of Chicago Press, 1992), p. 140.
3   *Ibid.*, p. 141.
4   E. Ringmar, *Identity, Interest, Action: A Cultural Explanation of Sweden's Intervention in the Thirty Years War* (Cambridge: Cambridge University Press, 1996), p. 69.
5   *Ibid.*, p. 70.
6   Amongst others, see M. Frost, 'Tragedy, Ethics and International Relations', *International Relations*, Vol. 17, No. 4 (2003), pp. 477–495; J. Mayall, 'Tragedy, Progress and International Order: A Response to Frost', *International Relations*, Vol. 17, No. 4 (2003), pp. 497–503.
7   K. Kotuv, *The Serbian Folk Epic: Its Theology and Anthropology* (New York: Philosophical Library, 1977), p. 13.
8   *Ibid.*, p. 14.
9   A. Johns-Putra, *The History of the Epic* (Houndmills: Palgrave, 2006), pp. 1–11.
10 There are many fragments and various tales which, when taken together, provide the epic story arc that informs Jason's journey with the Argonauts in search for the Golden Fleece. For a sample of these tales, see Robert Graves, *The Greek Myths: Volume Two* (Harmondsworth: Penguin Books, 1962), pp. 215–258.

11   A. D.Smith, 'Will and Sacrifice: Images of National Identity', *Millennium: Journal of International Studies*, Vol. 20, No. 5 (2001), p. 573.

12   K. Tololyan, 'Narrative culture and the motivation of the terrorist', in *Texts of Identity*, J. Shotter and K.J. Gergen (eds.) (London: Sage, 1998).

13   A representative sample could include, R. Brubaker, *Ethnicity Without Groups* (Cambridge: Harvard University Press, 2004); G. Duijzings, *Religion and the Politics of Identity in Kosovo* (New York: Columbia University Press, 2000); V. Bell, 'Historical Memory, Global Movements and Violence: Paul Gilroy and Arjun Appadurai in Conversation', *Theory, Culture and Society*, Vol. 16, No. 2 (1999), pp. 21–40.

14   N. Malcolm, *Kosovo: A Short History* (Macmillan: Basingstoke, 1998), p. 79.

15   *Ibid.*, p. 79.

16   *Ibid.*

17   A. Pennington and P. Levi, trans., *Marko The Prince: Serbo-Croat Heroic Songs* (Duckworth Press: London, 1984), p. 17.

18   T. Judah, *Kosovo: War and Revenge* (London: Yale University Press, 2002), pp. 48–49.

19   Cited in Judah, *Kosovo*, p. 49.

20   *Ibid.*, p. 45.

21   Helsinki Watch, *Yugoslavia: Crisis in Kosovo* (Helsinki Watch, March 1990), p. 23.

22   J. Mertus, *Kosovo: How Myths and Truths Started a War* (London: University of California Press, 1999), p. 109.

23   I. Andrić, *The Bridge Over the Drina* (London: Harvell Press, 1995), pp. 50–51.

24   Mertus, *Kosovo*, pp. 109–110.

25   *Ibid.*, p. 9.

26   H. Ram, *The Imperial Sublime: A Russian Poetics of Empire* (Madison, WI: University of Wisconsin Press, 2003), p. 215.

27   L. Tolstoy, *Hadji Murat* (Alexandria, VA: Orchises Press, 1996).

28   The phrase seeing things in a 'different light' stems from the recent interventions associated with the 'aesthetic turn' in IR. This turn has been led by the likes of Roland Bleiker, and draws on the work of others who have also engaged with poetics and global politics. A sample of writers including Stephen Chan, Roland Bleiker, Vivienne Jabri, Christine Sylvester and Chris Farrands touch on aesthetic IR, a move which should be explicitly differentiated from the nebulous body of writers who draw on popular sources, intertextualism or poststructuralism.

29   R. Barthes, *Empire of Signs* (London: Cape, 1983).

30   A. Belyi, 'Apokapilpsis v russkoi poe`zii', in *Republika* (Moscow: Simvolizm kak miroponimanie, 1994), pp. 409–410.

31   See *After 9/11* (2003), available: www.watsoninstitute.org/infopeace/after911/, accessed 20 September 2004.

32   S. Layton, 'A Russian Reverie: Chechnya's Literary Legacy', *History Today*, Vol. 47, No. 2 (1997), pp. 6–9.

33   *Ibid.*, p. 7.

34   J. Russell, 'Mujahideen, Mafia, Madmen ...: Russian Perceptions of Chechens during the Wars in Chechnya, 1994–1996 and 1999-to-Date', *Journal of Post-Communist Studies and Transition Politics*, Vol. 18, No. 1 (2002), pp. 73–96.

35 Ram, *The Imperial Sublime*, p. 9.
36 *Ibid.*, p. 208.
37 Stephen Chan and Peter Mandaville (eds.), *The Zen of International Relations* (London: Palgrave Macmillan, 2001), p. 9.
38 Ram, *The Imperial Sublime*, p. 11.
39 Layton, 'A Russian Reverie', pp. 113–114.
40 *Ibid.*, p. 111.
41 Ram, *The Imperial Sublime*, p. 11.
42 A. Field (ed.), 'Foreword', in *The Complection of Russian Literature* (Harmondsworth: Penguin, 1971), p. ix.
43 Unsurprisingly, this section of the story did not make it past the Russian censors before print.
44 L. Tolstoy, *The Raid and Other Stories* (Oxford: Oxford University Press, 1988), p. 22.
45 Human Rights Watch, Press Release, 'More Evidence of Rape by Russian Forces in Chechnya' (30 March 2000), www.hrw.org/press/2000/03/chech0330. htm; Amnesty International Report, 'Russian Federation: Chechen Republic "Normalization" in whose Eyes?' (23 June 2004), http://web.amnesty.org/library/ index/engeur460272004, all accessed 10 June 2005. Finally, see BBC News, 'Chechen Visit a Mixed Success' (4 April 2000), http://news.bbc.co.uk/1/hi/world/ europe/701590.stm.
46 Photo-Feature, 'Grozny: "An Internal" Russian Matter', *Index on Censorship*, Vol. 25 (1996), pp. 24–30, and 'Chechen Warning', pp. 31–32.
47 C. Gall and T. de Waal, *Chechnya: A Small Victorious War* (London: Pan, 1997), pp. 15–36.
48 D. Campbell, *National Deconstruction: Violence, Identity, and Justice in Bosnia* (London: University of Minnesota Press, 1991), p. 13.
49 K. Kurczab-Redlich, 'Torture and Rape Stalk the Streets of Chechnya', *The Observer* (Sunday 27 October 2002); Human Rights Watch, 'Russia/Chechnya—Swept Under: Torture, Forced Disappearances, and Extra-judicial Killings During Sweep Operations in Chechnya', Vol. 14, No. 2 (February 2002).
50 Human Rights Situation in Chechnya: Human Rights Watch Briefing Paper to the 59th Session of the UN Commission on Human Rights, United Nations (7 April 2003).
51 Russell, 'Mujahideen, Mafia, Madmen', pp. 73–96.
52 For instance, in February 2001 an unmarked grave was discovered at the Khankala military base where at least 60 corpses were found and this was expanded upon in a Human Rights Watch Report, which went on to say they had documented eight unmarked graves between 2000 and 2001. Human Rights Watch, 'Russia/ Chechnya: The Dirty War in Chechnya: Forced Disappearances, Torture, and Summary Executions', Vol. 13, No. 1 (March 2001), www.hrw.org/reports/2001/ chechnya/index.htm#TopOfPage.
53 Human Rights Watch Report (April 2004), 'Russia: Nine Civilians Extrajudicially Executed in Chechnya', http://hrw.org/english/docs/2004/04/12/russia8424.htm.
54 This is certainly the conclusion that Harsha Ram comes to in his analysis of the monographs by A. Lieven, *Chechnya: Tombstone of Russian Power* (New Haven,

CT: Yale University Press, 1998) and C. Gall and T. de Waal, *Chechnya: A Small Victorious War* (London: Pan Books, 1997). See H. Ram, 'Prisoners of the Caucasus: Literary Myths and Media Representations of the Chechen Conflict' (1999), http://ist-socrates.berkeley.edu/bsp/publications/1999_01-ram.pdf, accessed 15 May 2004.
55 Russell, 'Mujahideen, Mafia, Madmen', p. 97.
56 For example beyond the sources referenced in this chapter, see J. Colarusso, *Nart Sagas from the Caucasus: Myths and Legends from the Circassians, Abazas, Abkhaz, and Ubykhs* (Princeton, NJ: Princeton University Press); R. Elsie, *Albanian Literature: A Short History* (London: I.B. Tauris, 2005).

6

Criminality and war

So far this book has focused on a range of issues related to narrative and interpretive IR, as ways into analysing contemporary violence. In doing so, attention has been drawn to different levels of analysis, the role of history in the Caucasus and Balkans, and different social, cultural and local forms of identification. In both Kosovo and Chechnya we see contract soldiers, special police units and federal army units fighting against armed resistance movements. The armed resistance movements were, however, made up of a multiplicity of groups and networks, and this, alongside the role of NATO, the UN and other international organisations, problematise the way contemporary war is understood. This, in a sense, echoes the ideas established in work on 'new wars', when turning to 'decompression' and conflict. Thus conflicts may have a lot to do with warlordism, paramilitaries, militias and profiteering linking armed resistance to the black marketeers, criminal gangs and entrepreneurs of violence. However, another aspect of decompression of war is the criminalisation of violence – that is the labelling of irredentism as banditry by state authorities. In Kosovo and Chechnya, criminality and criminalisation combined.

To some extent, criminalising armed resistance movements produced the milieu in which different groups emerged, that sought to challenge the Serbian and Russian authorities. Of course lawlessness took markedly different forms – in Kosovo this led to the establishment of a 'ghost state' in the early 1990s and movements which advocated passive resistance – although the situation changed after the Dayton Peace Accords in 1995. In Chechnya after the first war, social unrest, economic depravation and political uncertainty created a darker period of lawlessness between 1997 and 1998. In a general sense then, both conflicts signal a movement away from the Western professionalised approach to war-fighting to a more nebulous and a somewhat more violent form of localised war, influenced by the centralisation of power and the development of a political culture in Russia and Serbia in the 1990s and by the processes of globalisation explored in Chapter 4.

The chapter is broken down into three sections, which are themselves further sub-divided. The chapter starts with an exploration of different groups in Chechnya in the period from 1996 through to early 1998, before turning to the changing dynamics of law enforcement in Russia and the mixture of Russian law enforcement organisations involved in the second conflict that erupted in 1999. The second part of the chapter turns to the emergence of the KLA from the 1980s into the 1990s, drawing attention to the wars in the Balkans in the 1990s, the Dayton Peace Accords which sought to bring an end to the war in Bosnia and the collapse of the state structures in Albania in 1997, before engaging with the formation of an armed resistance movement. The third section introduces the issue of multiple allegiances, so as to highlight, on the one hand, that local social groups underpinned the formation of the KLA and the Chechen armed resistance movements and, on the other hand, highlighting that local codes, indigenous traditions and norms are often masked by the general labelling of groups as criminals. Given the broader work on interpretive and storied identity, this section offers a bridge to the earlier work on stories of war and peace, indicating how this process of labelling afforded the threats in Kosovo and Chechnya to Serbia and Russia the status of internal issues. Some of these themes will be returned to in the following chapters.

Chechnya: the interregnum

In the months immediately after the first Russo-Chechen War of the 1990s, Aslan Maskhadov, in his capacity as Chief of Staff of the Chechen military during the conflict, gained widespread political support defeating Shamil Basayev and Zelimkhan Yandarbiyev, as well as Movladi Udugov in the post-war national elections on 27 January 1997. While negotiating with Russia on the principles of post-war Russo-Chechen independence, the newly elected Chechen President Maskhadov – a moderate and secular political leader – attempted to nullify the influence of indigenous Salafi groups by integrating them into the newly formed administration of the Chechen Republic of Ichkeria (ChRI). Islam Khalimov became the head of the Interior Ministry, which he immediately renamed the Ministry of Shar'ia Security (MSS), while Khalimov's deputies, Abdul-Malik Mezhidov and Supyan Abdullayev, were all linked to the Shar'ia Guard, an offshoot of the MSS which served a symbolic role as part of the Maskhadov administration. Somewhat surprisingly Maskhadov appointed Movladi Udugov as Foreign Minister, while

Yandarbiyev became a roving ambassador for the ChRI. For a short while then, the simmering tensions between Maskhadov's secular administration and advocates of Salafism remained in check.

Moderate elements in the Maskhadov administration were confronted with mounting internal problems in late 1997. Yandarbiyev, smarting from his defeat in the May elections, formed a parallel political organisation named the Caucasian Federation, while Dagestani and Chechen Islamists established the Islamic Nation Movement, forming a bridgehead to the Salafi group led by the Dagestani Islamist Bagautdin Magomedov.[1] Meanwhile the MSS sought ideological support from the Saudi Wahhabi spiritual adviser Abu Omar al-Sayf – a member of the Muslim Brotherhood – who had remained in the North Caucasus following the end of the first war. Abu Omar al-Sayf arrived in the North Caucasus in late 1995. He had worked as the spiritual advisor to Ibn Khattab, the leader of the Arab mujahideen in the latter part of the first Russo-Chechen war.[2] In 1995 Khattab used the military training and experience gained in Afghanistan and Tajikistan, to launch an ambush in Yarysh-Mardy as part of the broader Chechen war effort. The attack killed scores of Russian troops, establishing the military jamaat within the broader resistance movement, particularly given the significant military setbacks Chechen forces had suffered in that year. Khattab also had the ambush filmed and this quickly brought him to the attention of Shamil Basayev, who controlled the sector that the Khattab's jamaat operated within. Basayev invited Khattab to stay in Vedeno as his guest, and conferred on him the position of 'brother', a powerful symbolic gesture in Chechen customary tradition which simultaneously granted Khattab a measure of freedom and protection. Basayev's patronage cemented an alliance built on his and Khattab's respective military experiences: an alliance which gained momentum in the inter-bellum. These links to regional and international benefactors afforded the Salafi movement in Chechnya financial and theological support, partly due to al-Sayf's direct contact with Wahhabi Islamists in the Gulf States.

Throughout the later part of 1997, a loose coalition of people including Zelimkhan Yandarbiyev, Supyan Abdullayev, Movladi Udugov and Arbi Barayev – a notorious criminal from Urus-Martan – began to voice their discontent with the Maskhadov government. The younger generation of criminals associated with Arbi Barayev – himself a former bodyguard of Yandarbiyev – sought to consolidate their position in particular regions by embracing radical Salafism. In July 1997 Maskhadov signed a decree disbanding the plethora of militias and paramilitary groups loyal to wayward warlords that had appeared in the post-war period. The secondary aim was to create a professional Chechen army. While some warlords like Salman